ON ZELLER'S PRIOR BOOKS OF POETRY:

"Maya Jewell Zeller's poems reverberate in my heart long after I've read and heard them. From lines, sounds, and visions, she creates little worlds, and I can't wait to see this brilliant mind creating the full universe of a book-length narrative."

—ELISSA WASHUTA, author of *White Magic* and *My Body is a Book of Rules*

Y FERNS

MAYA JEWELL ZELLER

© 2026 by Maya Jewell Zeller

Published March 2026 by Porphyry Press
Post Office Box MXY via Glennallen
McCarthy, Alaska 99588
https://porphyry.press/

LIBRARY OF CONGRESS CATALOGING-IN-PUBLICATION DATA ON FILE
Library of Congress Control Number: 2025947664
First Edition
ISBN 978-1-7367558-7-7 (paperback)
ISBN 978-1-7367558-8-4 (e-pub)
ISBN 978-1-7367558-9-1 (audio)

Book design by Alban Fischer Design.
Text composed in Bulmer and Franklin Gothic
with Worker and Wheat for the display.
Author photo by Zoey Zeller.

All rights reserved. Except for brief quotations in critical articles or reviews, no part of this publication may be reproduced or transmitted in any form or by any means, electronic or mechanical, including photocopy, recording, or any informa-tion storage or retrieval system, without permission in writing from the publisher.

MORE PRAISE FOR *Raised by Ferns*

"A luminous meditation on growing up with empty pockets but a heart full of wildflowers, this memoir wanders barefoot through forests, riverbeds, and verses, gathering wisdom like stones. It's not about what was lacked, but what was found—in nature, in language, and in the quiet, never-ending act of becoming. I can't stop thinking about this book."

—JAMIE FORD, *New York Times* bestselling author of
Hotel on the Corner of Bitter and Sweet

"Not since Maggie Nelson's *The Argonauts* has someone redefined memoir so completely and beautifully as Maya Jewell Zeller does with *Raised by Ferns*. Zeller vividly recounts an itinerant childhood in the bracken and moss of Northwest watersheds, where the idea of 'home' was an elusive, shifting, mercurial landscape, and freedom and boundlessness were lauded over consistency and stability. The prose shifts between the registers of Zeller's original language—the language of lichen, rocks, and fern, of poverty, place, and self-reliance—with the registers she learns and masters and doubts, including those of the reluctant middle-class homeowner, the eloquent scholar, the accomplished author. This is a memoir unparalleled for its intelligence, its poetry, its self-awareness, its generosity, its critique of defined boundaries and binding definitions. No book has so thoroughly changed me as this one did: *Raised by Ferns* urges us to converse with our past selves and examine, mourn, and celebrate the ways in which they form the wondrous selves we are now."

—SHARMA SHIELDS, author of *The Cassandra*
and *Sasquatch Hunter's Almanac*

MORE PRAISE FOR *Raised by Ferns*

"I couldn't put *Raised by Ferns* down. Maya Jewell Zeller writes so beautifully about the deep difficulty of understanding oneself fully. Once a child growing up in precarity and now an adult trying to ethically navigate her privileged positions, she writes with honesty and insight about what it means to embrace all of the different versions of themselves a person has been. The author of the influential essay 'The Privilege Button,' in this memoir about growing up 'in a van by the river,' as her son once describes her childhood, Zeller shows readers what it means to belong to an earth that is always moving beneath our feet, terrifying in her unpredictable changing, but also springing forth new berries and fish and fiddlehead ferns that can sustain a family through this day and the next. A thoughtful consideration of the myriad forms childhood poverty can take and the impacts it can have, this is also a memoir about learning to love the wildly reckless, confused, and brave child she once was. What does it mean to have been the kind of kid who would run away by leaping from a moving van and the kind who would protect her little sister when their father's foreboding moods settled over the house? Beneath such a childhood's deep forest of shadows, surrounded by unfurling ferns, Zeller became the kind of woman who can write this book that shows us how to see the world around us in such beautiful, magical, compassionate, clear-eyed ways."

—**KATHRYN NUERNBERGER,** author of *The Witch of Eye*

For Raine

CONTENTS

ONE
The Privilege Button { 3
On a Beach in Oregon, 1970s Gas Shortage { 16
Barry's by the Sea { 25
Library/Van { 28
Scavenger Panorama { 33
Sestina for Foragers { 44
Poverty Fires { 51
Complete the Sentence { 58

TWO
Maslow's Hierarchy of Needs { 77
Everything I Know About "Ordinary and Typical Human Beings Who Made it Into Heaven" I Learned from the Movie *Saint Ralph* { 103
Balsamroot's Arrow-Shaped Leaves Point in So Many Directions at Once { 106
He Worked as an Electrician. He Enjoyed Television. (His Obituary Was Plain.) { 114
Letters to Francesca Woodman from Spokane and Farther West { 121
"Napoleon is So Small and His Horse is So Huge" { 127
Where My Mother Never Set Foot { 139

THREE

Landscape Anxiety { 151
Ruin Porn { 164
The Metamorphosis { 182
How to Trespass { 197
Raised by Ferns { 209

EPILOGUE: *The Privilege (Un)Button*

Blue Tongue { 225

ACKNOWLEDGMENTS { 245
NOTES { 249

*I am so hungry
for the song that grows tall like a weed
grows, and grows.*

—DIANE SEUSS

There is a woman's veil shrunk to a religion of brown.

—MELISSA KWASNY

ONE

THE PRIVILEGE BUTTON

A young poet with low elite-culture literacy walks into a wine bar and scans the menu, not sure what to order. She's trying to come off as sophisticated—after all, she holds an advanced degree—but wine bars make her nervous, because she has never heard most of the menu items pronounced out loud. She finds something that sounds simple and familiar enough—she knows well what wild things a hungry person can eat. Rose hips are high in vitamin C, and they make a bittersweet, earthy tea. The poet says loudly, confidently, "I'll have the RŌSE," pronouncing it like the flower, one syllable, with a long *o*.

"What's that?" asks the bartender, assuming he misheard.

Her friend leans in, interjecting. "*She'll have the rosé.*"

"Right," the poet says, blushing. "That's what I meant."

When the wine comes, it does not taste like roses. This is because it is drawn from the skin of fermenting red grapes. Named for its color, it has nothing to do with flowers.

*

When I was a child, I dreamed of a literary life. I could feel it when I read poetry—"the dark spirit of the earth coming up," as Spanish poet Federico García Lorca would say, "through the soles of the feet."

Wrote Lorca: "One must awaken the duende in the remotest mansions of the blood."

My blood is more like a trailer park.

This is the story of how I came to live in an HOA, an acronym you may know; but in case you, too, were ever flustered at a dessert menu and had to look up how to pronounce *ganache*, HOA stands for "homeowners' association," which is governed by a set of rules for neighborhood living.

*

> **Fairwood Park II HOA, Article II—Protective Covenants, Section 2.04—Temporary Structures:**
> No trailer, basement, tent, shack, garage, barn, camper or other outbuilding or any structure of temporary character erected or placed on the property shall at any time be used as a residence.

When we first moved to Spokane, my husband and I lived in a 1912 house near West Central. We pulled weeds, planted lilacs, phlox, and fruit trees. We put plastic on our old windows to keep out the cold, and when, that first January, the temperature dropped into the negatives for over a week, we used a hair dryer to thaw the uninsulated pipes that ran too close to the foundation wall. We tried wrapping them, too, but it seemed their freezing was inevitable. There were things about the house that we couldn't fix, and we loved it for those things.

I always felt rich there, and I thought our $100,000 loan was a fortune. We were *homeowners*! Or, at least, could be if we made our payments. I was still baffled by the notion of a permanent address. My parents had been renters, even squatters; sometimes, we lived in a garage. Sometimes, we lived in a van. When I repeated this to my husband, years into marriage, he shook his head and said, with a realization I hadn't reached (and still resist), "Maya, you were homeless."

I had never thought of myself as homeless. *Itinerant*, maybe, *gypsy*, sure—I didn't yet know the term's problematic usage. Not *homeless*. More like a mouse after a flood, finding a new place for its nest.

We made those nests in rural areas, where we ate salmon my brother caught from the river, blackberries we picked in the fields. We always had some kind of roof, a basin, a woodstove. We usually went to school, and we visited the library.

My mother sang Cher's "Gypsies, Tramps, and Thieves" while she darned our socks, and my father hummed "King of the Road" when, two beers into the night, he still felt jolly. Sometimes my father drove a tow truck and filled the bushes around us with junked cars, treasure troves where we discovered free cassette tapes(!) and cool T-shirts(!). The cars were playhouses, magic passageways to other lives, fuel to dreams of a future in which I would be sophisticated enough to attend fancy fundraisers in ornate buildings. I dreamed these things the way a child dreams them, without any real awareness of my family's economic status, without any shame of it.

> **Section 2.05—Minimum Dwelling Cost:** No single family dwelling shall be permitted on any lot at a cost of less than $100,000 exclusive of land.

When I began college in the late '90s, the socioeconomic privilege of my peer cohort was often taken for granted by my instructors, who said things like, "Well, *we* can't really understand, being middle class." They used words like *cul-de-sac* and *IRA* and sometimes made cultural references from TV shows like *Seinfeld* and channels like CNN. They said "The Dow is down two points"; I kept my eyes low. I didn't really know what middle class meant, though I'd been passing so far. When I took a course in the culture of poverty as it related to education and language register, I finally understood: I grew up "in poverty," "in a family of addiction." But I knew how to move between formal and informal language registers, so no one picked up on my past. Still, I was what we were studying: How to move from a culture of poverty into a culture of education. How to serve an at-risk population, students with family lives like mine: cycles of addiction, impermanent addresses, free and reduced lunches. In discussion, my classmates often said things like "I had no idea so many people in America lived like this," or "I never realized poverty could be so beyond your control."

I kept quiet; I was not interested in being a lab rat. I was not interested in changing, in their view, from a competent, assertive person I'd worked so hard to become to an anomaly of class transcendence. How many questions would follow? They were questions I did not feel comfortable answering.

I still don't.

*

I'd always thought of suburbs with some measure of disdain. Suburbs were those places where children had bicycles from the time they were small, where fathers never came home drunk or yelled at the moon, where there were Christmas lights and where Santa always brought gifts, and where people believed it *was* Santa—those places so many of my peers in college imagined just meant America. As I grew into my developing adult identity as part of the working middle class, I held less disdain, but I never coveted that world. Materially, I felt comfortable in our first home—it felt like enough. I was with the people, my people. There were renters among us; there were people who didn't water their lawns; people who didn't shovel their sidewalks; cars on blocks; tiny homes with large gardens; the occasional woman walking down the street with her garbage bag of clothes—I'd go out and see if she needed a ride to the shelter or a bus ticket to somewhere better than where she'd been, to a relative, maybe, a friend. I stood at my fence with my baby on my hip and I talked with Richard from across the street. He reminded me of my father: he said *shit* a lot, even in front of my little one, and when he developed an infection and abscess in his foot, we drove to Walgreens to buy his iodine ointment, kept watch over his place while he was in the hospital hitting on Wendy, his nurse. And there was a recent trend to have block parties; our neighbor Dave started a community garden, a farmers' market. The neighborhood hummed with a sense of community, a little dirt in the cracks.

Lately, though, we'd had nightly break-ins to our car, and the sirens screaming by all hours of the day made me constantly anxious. I'd never acclimated fully to city living. I couldn't adjust to how close we were to major roads, our house viewable by Google satellites, the tree cover too thin. We joked that we probably should not grow pot in our garden among the tomatoes, even if we wanted to (this was before legalization in Washington State). Outside our oasis of a yard, our children would grow up mostly playing on pavement, with the neighborhood kids who roamed freely, like quail, down the block. Would our children miss the fields they didn't know? Could we bring the woods to their door?

We calculated the economic reality. We weren't debt free, but we were frugal, and we both had decent, working-class jobs. It was 2014—the housing market not yet bananas. I was teaching, as a non-tenured instructor for more than one college; my husband coached cross-country and track for a university—it didn't pay well, but it paid ($17K at the time, half what I made total from my multiple adjunct positions). After nine years, we didn't owe much on our house; we'd paid down our loan quickly. So we could afford to move to this beautiful home outside of town. I had never dreamed of living in a suburb, but suddenly, after five years teaching at a university, I wanted to, and a small part of me, the part of which I somehow felt ashamed, felt I was entitled to live away from daily crime. Did my entitlement grow out of the privilege (the security?) I'd managed to sustain?

> **Fairwood Park II HOA, Article II—Protective Covenants, Section 2.06—Minimum Dwelling Specifications:** The ground floor area of the main structure, exclusive of open porches, and garages, shall not be less than one thousand (1,000) square feet for a one-story dwelling, no less than eight hundred (800) square feet for the ground floor area of a dwelling of more than one story. All dwellings shall have enclosed garages of at least 20 feet by 22 feet, with completely sealed interior, walls and ceilings, and with fully paved driveways to the street.

My husband and I discussed. Should we move from one perfectly acceptable home to another? To say I was torn would be understatement. The modernist poet Wallace Stevens would say I was "of two minds": part of me still hated money, hated to think of myself as the person who had it. The other part of me dreamed of quiet, the illusion of safety, a yard where my children could roam, naked. Was that too much to ask? Should any one person have that when everyone else cannot? I spent nights agonizing. I had metaphoric narrative nightmares. I woke sure I was a sellout. I thought of how, just a few years ago, I'd applied for unemployment. Though we were homeowners, we lived in an area of town where everyone struggled. I realized that struggle was part of my identity, poverty was part of my identity, and moving would be admitting finally that I'd shifted in social class, whatever that meant.

E. D. Hirsch, a conservative educational theorist who influenced national policies during the Reagan administration, writes in his book *Dictionary of Cultural Literacy* about "combating the social determinism that condemns [children] to remain in the same social and educational condition as their parents." I'd mastered a good degree of cultural literacy; my membership had shifted, leaving behind the identity of my "disadvantaged" and "at-risk" youth. I realized this with a degree of bitterness: many of the most positive aspects of my childhood, the things that had shaped me, were due to those less-than-acculturated circumstances. Days of unsupervised play, roaming the fields and forests, a dependent reliance on the public library (which afforded me a range of literary tastes and, admittedly, a small degree of American culture awareness), the ability to create a meal from scratch using limited ingredients, knowing what wild plants were edible (surely not in Hirsch's *Dictionary of Cultural Literacy?*), a sense of empathy for others who had less, and a realization that you have to work hard for what you have and take care of it. I wondered: could a person sustain a working-class sensibility of the world and—more importantly—instill it not as theory but as practice in her children if they lived in a social bubble?

Also, there was the commute factor. The move would change my commute from two miles to twelve; that was just for my work, not to mention my husband's job, and my involvement as a literary citizen in the downtown community. Moving would increase our carbon footprint, decrease leisure time.

And the house was unnecessarily large—four bedrooms, a third bathroom (laughable to me, how unnecessary, how convenient). And a sprinkler system! And a doorbell! Two ovens! A two-car garage, with automatic opener! Some of the common areas between houses even had their own pools. All of these frivolities!

Still, I wanted it. *We* wanted it. We were tired of the city. My husband had grown up in the suburbs; I in rural places. The neighborhood of the new home was close to Fish & Wildlife land, with bald eagles and moose and a river. Our children could have access to "nature"—to the kinds of places my siblings and I spent our formative years.

In town, we'd kept a garden, but now I imagined our long walks through the crumbled homestead and defunct dairy farm that made up part of the valley adjacent to the neighborhood. We might find an old apple tree, a field full of edible plants. When I was a child, I sometimes roamed all day, eating what was edible when I was hungry, coming home only when I was tired, my clothes stained with plums or salmonberry, my pockets full of fossils from the riverbeds, of petrified chunks of wood from the clay banks in the forest beyond. My siblings and I had memorized the maps to treasures only a rural, roaming child can find: not Barbies but blackberries, not piano lessons but the steady beat of rain on a tin roof, the glinting rhythm of salmon fins fighting their way upstream.

My husband, a trained capitalist, saw moving as the next step in our forward progress. He grew up middle class, to parents with a working-class upbringing, whose expression of security meant acquiring new material possessions. So after the fantasizing and the agonizing and the measured discussions, we agreed to move from one dream to another, and we promised each other that we would remain frugal, not fall into materialism or other values outside ourselves, not take comfort for granted, not to waste it or to become too American. We promised each other we'd remain grateful for our privilege. It was like another kind of marriage: admitting the merge we'd become, his youth-group-president upbringing with my feral youth.

*

After careful deliberation, frugal living, and in accordance with the standard social mobility of the educated middle class, our family moved from our starter home into a four-bedroom, three-bath house in a well-established neighborhood, north of town, with a half-acre yard and HOA bylaws. I was nervous about acclimating to these new, strange rules, but I had also grown weary and anxious in town, and I looked forward to the quiet of stars.

At our first HOA meeting, people were welcoming, but some felt furious about the Smiths, converting their one-family home into a shared living space for their parents and elderly friends ("Three families in one house? Who heard of such a thing? There'll be cars coming and going all hours of the day!"). They also ranted about the apartments, just beyond our HOA boundary, that were transitioning to low-income, government housing. I pick up a subtext: Do not, under any circumstances, tell us you grew up in poverty. This breaks Section 2.08, Exterior Maintenance, which stipulates, among other things, you must always keep a clean curb.

*

For several years, I taught writing at a private liberal arts institution, a school known for its basketball teams, its Jesuit tradition, and its students' relative privilege. (There are students on full scholarship, from Washington apple country, urban areas, or small Montana towns who navigate a sense of culture shock and a socioeconomic gap even wider than the one I charted at a state school.) In my first year of adjunct work at this private university, where at the time my salary was less than my students' tuition, I approached the topic by teaching Barbara Ehrenreich's *Nickel and Dimed*, in which she works as a Merry Maid. When students expressed surprise at the maids' working conditions, of the meager American dream offered to someone employed full-time, or when they made statements about how a person could "pull themselves out of it" if they "get a degree," I asked how many of their families employed maids; half the class raised their hands. After their awkward glances and equivocations, I shared that to put myself through college I worked as a custodian, changing sheets and cleaning dorm showers of high school football campers who, mostly oblivious to who replaced their towels, would sometimes prank us by shitting in the shower or behind the beds.

My students went back to their dorms and cleaned their own toilets; they ventured into Spokane on city buses, many of them using public transportation for the first time in their lives. In reflective research essays, they referenced these experiences, a range of statistics, Ehrenreich and other authors, and the university's social justice mission. But it was still difficult to help those sweet young people—many of whom, since the age of sixteen, had driven their own cars (cars in which they did not also live)—understand how hard work does not necessarily equal a fair shot.

As is the case with many of us raised in (and out of) economic poverty, as an adult with some economic stability, I often feel guilt. At the private university, I rarely admitted this to my students. I also didn't tell them that Barbara Ehrenreich's anthropological experiment made me personally angry, that her immersion in poverty for the sake of narrative journalism felt like exploitation, that I always feared the essays I assigned might skirt appropriation. The entire time Ehrenreich worked undercover as a journalist, she held a bank account on which she could fall back and had health insurance she could access. She did not have to make any hard choices; for her, there was a clear end to poverty. I understand what she was doing, though: passing. Playing a role.

Fairwood Park II HOA, Article II—Protective Covenants, Section 2.15—Animals: No animal, livestock or poultry of any kind may be raised, bred, or kept on any lot.

In Spokane, as in many cities across the nation, urban chickens are a large part of the neighborhood experience. Within the last several years, our city passed an ordinance that increased fowl allotment from three hens to five (no roosters). But in Fairwood Park II, the covenants forbid this use of your land.

We want chickens, but we decide to wait it out.

Then there was an opening on the HOA board and my husband became president. He and another at-large member (whose wife is an artist; she grew up on twenty acres, unschooled) talked about infiltrating the ranks and working toward modifying that covenant to allow people to keep birds.

We all knew we were mostly joking, though. It would take a quorum of 75 percent to change a covenant, and those opposed have been here since the beginning; they've built their little suburban utopia, and nothing is going to take it from them. Frankly, we're not even sure how to begin this conversation, among the talk of blocking off the end of our neighborhood so "those low-income apartments don't have access" and the big to-do over one woman's "garden art" that other residents find offensive.

> **Fairwood Park II HOA, Article II—Protective Covenants, Section 2.11—Fences:** Fences shall be well constructed of suitable fencing materials and shall be artistic in design and shall not detract from the appearance of the dwelling house located upon the adjacent lots or building sites or be offensive to the owners or occupants thereof.

*

My navigation of this world is still tenuous. I don't always pronounce words correctly, and I don't fully understand middle-class social cues. I sometimes make generalizations, like "Many people who grow up with money don't understand they have money." (My children may be these people. No matter how much I ask them to reflect, they cannot yet fathom that the amount we spend each month for piano lessons is the equivalent of what my family once paid monthly in rent.)

I am deeply grateful for my life's security, tenuous as I know it to be, but the irony of my relative socioeconomic extravagance and the existence of systems that privilege my particular literacy and race does not escape me. When I drive home from work in my functional car, past the No Soliciting signs at the neighborhood entrance, the deer grazing in yards, where programmed sprinkler systems water the plants, when I pull into my "fully paved driveway," I reach up to my sun visor and press the button on my automatic garage door opener. Like magic, the door glides up. I call the garage door opener "the privilege button," and every time I push it, I shake my head, giggle to myself.

I laugh, but I also tell the story to my students, where I now teach, at a state school. I tell them I want to believe if we communicate thoughtfully across our intersectional advantages and disadvantages, we might bridge some boundaries. I tell them I still need to work on my daily actions, my hypocrisies—we all do.

I tell them that when I push the privilege button, my garage door glides up to reveal a very human, middle-class mess: kayaks stacked on cement blocks, bicycles and scooters piled on a lawn mower, old tires still in their bags, an unplugged refrigerator, a workbench covered with tools and manila folders, crates of books, a box of childhood treasures, old cassette tapes. They're safe and warm here in this "completely sealed interior."

The door that conveniently leads directly from garage to house opens and out spill two giddy children, their faces sticky with melon juice. They've been practicing piano, building worlds that lead to Narnia. They're learning to say words in more than one language, they're learning what code-switching means, and they're learning they must practice empathy, be mindful when they push their privilege buttons. They have big dreams and finely tuned senses of humor. And on the off chance we someday find ourselves in an expensive restaurant, they'll probably laugh kindheartedly at their mom, who still won't be sure if she got it right: ganache. Guanache? Whatever.

ON A BEACH IN OREGON, 1970s GASOLINE SHORTAGE

I was born in a gas station on the Oregon Coast, and my parents paid the midwives with wool blankets and gasoline.

This is how it began. Nine months pregnant, mid-July, my midwestern mother walked the trail to the ocean, her belly so big she couldn't see her feet. Behind her, the long gray ribbon of Highway 101, or a thread from ribbons, looping through the eye of the Arch Cape tunnel, all along the ravel of coast, that seam of road stitching the sea and sky together with the land.

Behind the road, the scrap of acreage where my parents made their life—that gas station they called home—where maybe you can hear my toddler brother yelling for the cat, chasing the chickens. And behind the gas station and chickens, the hills of cedar and fir, the tangle of salmonberry blossom and the trilling bloomsong of thrush in spring; heavy, fat blackberries in late summer, and rain all the year round. And the morning fog spreading its smoothing blanket all the way from the lumps of hills to the salty ocean, and that ocean lapped the shore like the edge of a wool throw on a mattress, those threads of surf stretching and reaching toward the smoothed-over rocks. Like a bed someone has tossed in, risen from, near sunset.

My mother, in labor so long she finally left her room, did what she knew to do: She walked away from the green hills and gas rationing and probably still-fervent throngs of unserved customers whose needs she could not meet, even if she wasn't in that moment thrumming with a child unsure whether it wanted to rush out or to stay in, a child unaware of what angers the world held for her. My mother roamed across the highway's ache of cars and down the small footpath, past dune grass and shore pine and gulls and bees, along the rocks and the brown-green sparkle of creek to the arches that mark that edge of where people live.

She carried unborn-me, still-curled me, to where mussels and anemones and sea stars and sculpins dart and burrow into their homes.

Where the creek's fresh hill waters meet the tide, in the shadow of the fern-covered hill, my mother walked into the sea, all the way to her waist, and stood, rocking. "It was a full moon," she tells me, "and I was so tired!" And when I ask with my eyes about fear—the ocean, the night, the aloneness—"But no, I wasn't afraid. I asked the tide to pull you out of me." The moon was there, and all the rest. Can you imagine. Moving, in full exhausted labor, into the sea. She must have felt so strange, and so strangely alive.

She returned the way she came, walking the quarter mile, the shell-strewn path, back to the gas station, and into the bed where she says, soon after the spell she wove with that walk down on the moon-beach, I was born.

My father returned home just in time. My father, who'd been in Guatemala eking out a living by bringing blankets home, now that the gas supply was so low. Wool blankets, from Mayan people who knew he was about to be a father again. My father—German

American, raised in military barracks outside of Darmstadt, with his German mother, Carmen, and his American father, Marvin, coming to America only after he grew up an outcast, speaking his mother's language and the guttural crude English of his father, landing at last here in the Pacific Northwest, where he found finally something like *zuhause*—my father who notes he often "felt like an immigrant in his own country." Part of me wants to believe he understood the Mayan people whose handwork he sold because they, too, came from a history of feeling displaced. Another part of me says, "Except they're Indigenous, and he's not." Part of me will never fully understand my father, born in Ueberau, brought here and expected to thrive like a naturalized blackberry, who lived on the streets in Virginia after his mother died, spent his teens in and out of boys' detention centers, who milked cows to skip the war, who a decade later made a little quilt scrap of a life with my midwestern mother.

It was the 1970s, the Carter administration had asked Americans to ration gasoline, and my father carried the whole unexamined history of America with him to that service station, struggling to root in, driving back through Mexico, so he could feed his toddler son, his almost-born daughter.

*

In the summer of 1979, my father drove back from Guatemala with a van full of wool blankets he would sell in flea markets, or out of our gas station, for ten dollars each. Except those he and my mother gave to the midwives for assisting with my birth.

Among the sparse collection of material possessions that moved with us from place to place—a potted yucca, my father's briefcase of papers and photos, and a few sentimental pottery bowls—I held onto and still have one of these blankets—white, light blue, and pink, woven in a falsa stripe design—in my closet. When my father comes to visit, he mistakes my blanket as one of his own, and my mother reminds him, "No, Barry, that's Maya's—you gave it to her when she was a girl."

"Ohhhh—" he says, bewildered like an old man. Then, "No—that one's mine. I brought it with me." They go around a while like that before he concedes and leaves the blanket.

To avoid confusion, and to claim it as mine—a token of object/psychological permanence, perhaps—I take the blanket to my apartment in a town three hours away, where I teach at the university. Commuting back and forth between Spokane and Ellensburg, I contribute to the fossil fuel problem, and "living alone" in my second residence—for those first two years, a one-bedroom apartment—feels frivolous to me, but also like a sort of warped cellular destiny: the split identity, the bifurcated life. Half of me back in childhood, half of me here. Half of me chasing my brother and chickens across the mud and through the salt air outside a gas station, half of me walking the polished brick avenues of the university, wandering the sculptures and the art museum and Japanese gardens and the library.

Let me try again: I was born in the studio apartment (a generous term) above my parents' tiny coastal gas station in the 1970s, and my parents paid the midwives with gasoline and blankets from Mexico. I was told beautiful stories of how my name—*Maya Jewell*—came to be, and I believed them. I believed in the striped myths they wove, of Identity and Off-Grid Life and Immigration and Emigration and Ocean-Based Birth Magic and Other Stories. I believed them until I didn't, until each piece of me began to feel like something my parents had fabricated, a story that wasn't really mine. They made realities the ways we all do—to name What's Real, What's True, What's Worth Retelling, to ourselves and to others around us. I spent my childhood living in various rural places, staying/sleeping in various shelters—in apartments attached to the latest doomed business venture, in vans, trailers, a garage, a farmhouse with the bathtub falling through the floor, a tiny home that belonged to my mother's brother, a duplex in a neighborhood, a converted bus, a farmhouse full of ghosts, a house with an attic full of mice, a van in the parking lot, a van parked up a service road, a campground with reduced rates. A van made up like a story, or a poem, or a hybrid verse, with metaphors you could climb inside and pretend were stanzas, strophes, whole rooms in repeated or different shapes with hallways and pictures on the walls.

*

These are those stories: the moon, the river, the drive from Guatemala back to the Oregon Coast. A journal with a homemade cover: postage stamps.

I tell and tell again my story: I was born at the confluence of the Arch Cape Creek, the Pacific Ocean, the tunnel, the tangle of three kinds of blackberries—two introduced/naturalized species and one native.

The objective correlative here is easily spelled out: the blackberries are obviously invasive but naturalized, as my parents might have been; and I arrived beautifully, *naturally*, a jewel, they said, under a full moon—except every story contains shifting lines.

I want to ask myself, Which of the following aren't true? as a way to interrogate my own mythos. Of course, once it roots into you, truth becomes subjective. Which of the following weren't *always* true?

My mother had been married, once—
My father had been in love.

My mother's father, a Teamster, was always on the road.

My father's mother, Carmen, died of cancer, which is why my father moved to America.

My father's mother, Carmen, held false documents that helped her escape during World War II. This is what my sister and I wonder when looking through our father's briefcase full of passports and birth certificates. Carmen's don't always match—they have different dates, different ages. What was her real name? Why did she really marry Marvin, an American soldier? Who was her eldest son's father?

The Himalayan blackberry came to the United States from Eurasia in 1885, and it spread into the hills.

The Himalayan blackberry was introduced to Germany in 1835.

Cancer spreads not like a military but like a blackberry.

Blackberry spreads like a cancer.

Cancer isn't militant so much as fruitful—it produces globules of black gold.

The globules of berries are not unlike the beads of sand on my fingers while I eat berries on the beach near where I was born.

The sand in Arch Cape produces hours of easy recreation for small children.

My five-year-old son: "Ohhhh, I thought a honeymoon is when the moon was yellow."

Me, upon learning I was born under a gibbous moon: "Oh, I thought the moon was full—"

Me, upon learning the tide schedule for July __, 1979 (is this even my birthday? When order falls away from the world and your parents file for a birth certificate when you are two years old, how can you know any of the details are accurate?): *Oh, the tide was not high. The tide was low. The shells were exposed.*

In the 1980s, the tide pools near the beach of my birth were covered in sea anemones and sea stars.

Thirty years later, I cannot find a single sea star.

The anemones are limp in the warm water.

A whale carries her dead baby for nineteen days off the coast of Washington, just north of here.

When my son was born, he was blue.

When I was born, I tore my mother open, and she needed thirteen stitches.

I had to make up the number of stitches.

My forehead is stitched where a plate—a wild child's Frisbee—cut it open when I was four. The scar is crescent-shaped and comes out when I'm hot and red in the face.

I am hot and red in the face when I run.

I run when I'm overwhelmed and anxious.

The summer after I begin my tenure-track job, commuting three hours to another town and staying away from my children for several nights to earn the living that keeps them and my spouse in the dreamhouse, me struggling with anxiety and insomnia, feeling displaced and split, I finally seek therapy (for the first time in my life). I see the therapist only three times, until he asks if my current condition is recurring: "What did you do when you were a child and had to cope with pain and anxiety?"

Now I know what I was doing was my own version of what we all do: fight and flight.

Fight was to beat the blackberry bushes senseless with the golf club I found in the fields after the flood.

Flight was when I packed my mother's Iowa suitcase and ran away into the woods, to live in the arch of an old-growth cedar where I liked to watch the rain run down in rivulets and make small maps of our watershed, the last one before the ocean.

Before the ocean, a delta is a place where toxins murk and bloom. It's the last thing before the ocean.

A delta is a confluence of many forces: gasoline, salt, microbacteria, and life—so much life at the confluence of fresh and ocean water. So much room for fecundity.

A delta is like breast milk.

Breast milk is the best milk.

I know I was born in a gas station on the Oregon Coast in 1979 and my German-born father, just returned from Mexico, paid the midwives with blankets and gasoline. My mother lay in the ocean salt of the sea—where she'd waded after a day of labor—and the body salt of my amniotic fluid, and she nursed me. I drank and I cried and I gazed at the world, knowing nothing. The moon was gibbous and the ocean was hushing, was thrashing quietly, across the highway. In the greenhouse the marijuana grew taller than my brother. I knew nothing but the shifting of sound from thumps to crashes. I know less now.

BARRY'S BY THE SEA

For the first two years of my life, I was raised in that gas station off Highway 101, south of Cannon Beach and north of Manzanita. My parents named their business Barry's by the Sea. The upstairs apartment, reached by reclaimed-wood-turned-stairs, also had a hole in the plywood floor, which my father cut with a chainsaw, above the gas station's woodstove, so the heat could warm the second story, sawdust and wood dust mixing with the smell of ocean and the sound of robinsong floating in and around the tub they somehow hauled up and placed near the sawed-out window, fit with some glass scrap from a junkyard. It was how my parents did construction: upcycling before upcycling was chic—a chicken coop made from found parts, signs painted on scrap wood, *GAS*, in bright red letters. They heated water on the old woodstove in the back of the station and carried it up to the tub, where my mother bathed me and my older brother, and, once we were clean, herself—a square photo from this time shows her, bright breasts caught in half-profile, her arms up, washing her hair, brown eyes looking out into mottled dawn light. There's a fog to the photo, what the 1970s often looks like in my mind: that dream of a life they had, hardship and hope, marijuana and the decadence of Sarah Jo's caramels their friends Tom and Nancy made at home in a tall candy pot on their kitchen stove, the sweet, tawny treat the color of their linoleum floor, cut and twisted up in plastic wrap, sold to tourists in novelty shops and people driving the American dream, stopping for gas and nostalgia, to meet the "free spirits" who ran this little coastal town or their wild children dotting the land, learning birds and shells, and always the wash of cars and sea merging so the rush of one and the rush of the other—highway, shore—blur and blend like memory.

Behind the gas station, in the blackberry canes, they built their small poultry run, though the photos show the chickens—like the children—wandering the property, my brother running after the birds, calling *bawk bawk* or sitting with a board book on the mud-grass ground, a hen pecking nearby, a cat creeping out of the green thatch. I'm in a secondhand pram, my mother in jeans or corduroy, a flannel, and old work boots. She's thin and gazing west, across the highway toward the surf.

From the aerial, our gas station looks like a small smear of paint and metal near the Arch Cape tunnel, and by the time I'm old enough to begin to understand any of this, they've sold it—and the buyer, not into scavenger-kitsch, burns the building to the ground—and we're driving to central Oregon, where they'll open another gas station, in a small scoria-pocked non-town near a river, and that one will also go out of business, a sister will be born, winter is snow and cold floors and oatmeal and an outhouse, summer is hot lava rock and garden and hose water and mostly naked and pine cones, and we'll move—in our van—back to the coast, and we'll crash in a vacant rental for two weeks, where I'll enroll in kindergarten just long enough to learn how to navigate hallways and lunch rooms and then leave again, and we'll be on the road to Iowa, and we'll crash in some maternal uncle's empty house, and then we'll go again, back to Oregon, and then to Washington, some small town on a river or in a valley where the floods come, the gulls come, the seals, the sea lions,

ions, beer buzz, hiccup, fever, the siblings and nettles and bud scales on rhododendrons or azaleas the most reliable recurring knowns.

My life was never linear, never a narrative through line, school was something we did when it was convenient, and learning a constant tangle of curiosity and briar. We learned blossom and library, seasons and fear, hunger and quiet and hurry and pack, and that worry is inevitable, and love is complicated, that comfort and lessons can both sting and sing.

My father used to tell stories of how, as a teen, he lived on the streets and stole turkeys, turned in scrap metal for cash, and my mother related how her eight siblings always followed the rules in the house where there was a girls' room and a boys' room, four children in each, their narrow beds like the children in a *Madeline* book, their good shoes and ironed clothes and Catholic Mass. We were some blend of those beginnings: My father spoke loudly in the mornings and loudly in the evenings and when he was gone, working, my mother read us books and taught us to bake bread. I learned early the advantage of keeping my opinions to myself, and then later to be heard I'd have to yell them and then hide in my room or go to the barn or river. I learned to search for patterns and shape them to my advantage. Learned to treat myself as my own best friend, to be scrappy as a half-kept bird, wandering the landscape around a gas station, looking for seed. I learned the land loves you back, and the land doesn't always love you back, and that if you fail, you just go somewhere else to start over. And I learned that the existence of libraries and books, and what happens in spring with dormant sticks turning to blossoms and leaves, means there is always a future, and you can hold the past inside yourself like a little doll.

LIBRARY / VAN

Wherever my family lived after that, it wasn't a town.

It was a series of back roads off Highway 101, or 97, or the Columbia River Highway, or State Route 4 ... a river bend tourists would have driven past—or did—if it wasn't for their interest in the covered bridge, promised like a Meryl Streep movie, if you take the turn indicated and head down the hill, past the tangle of maple and alder, sword fern and salmonberry, through the field of hay grass and thistle with the nettled edge.

I didn't know what a rom-com was or much about culture beyond our valleys. But once a week, my mother took us to the library van in Naselle, a fifteen-minute drive from where we rented an old farmhouse in Grays River. I thought of that van the way I imagine some kids in cities might anticipate the ice cream truck—at first, with excitement over their new flavors. I could almost taste the books—and soon, with awareness, having devoured every kind, intoning which I would choose based on my mood, the color and definition of clouds. It wasn't long before I had read every children's book in the van and moved on to YA, then adult.

The van of books was part of the Timberland Regional Library System (TRLS). TRLS libraries serve the five southwest Washington counties of Grays Harbor, Thurston, Mason, Lewis, and Pacific. In the late 1980s, before TRLS expanded to the twenty-nine-library network it sustains today, they utilized Bookmobiles—vans stationed in the most rural of rural communities so children like me could check out materials.

The library van was a small castle of knowledge, imagination, possibility. Like my natural library of flora, the van held both familiarity and the promise of something beyond that familiarity. When I think of libraries, I think of vans. I think of my other kind of "library van"—the kind that happened when my family left that valley I knew and drove away in a VW bus made up like a small home on wheels, traveled every couple months to make a little cash so we could keep paying our cheap ($150 a month) rent, keep living in the farmhouse with the bathtub falling through the floor and the fields and fields and brambles and sky and river.

* * *

I'm ten. It's summer, or more specifically, a summer-like fall. Our parents have pulled us from school again, and I'm at a library in Winlock, in Raymond, in Shelton, in Elma, in Hoquiam. It doesn't matter which one. Whichever it is, I know this library. They are all over southwest Washington, in all the rural towns of the Willapa Hills. My mother and father leave my sister and me at the library (how so many of us now leave our children with screens), while they (my parents and thirteen-year-old brother) re-cover billiards tables.

For an hour or so, we sit obediently in the stacks, reading children's books to one another, exploring the magical realms of endless language. But we're children, so we wander . . . like our library van, searching for more library vans, for curious lands, our hands curious and searching for curiosities.

In one town, we find a bank with a fountain.

The fountain is full of coins!

What a joy for two children whose books are loans, whose toys are whistle-grass and bull thistle, who live sometimes-itinerant lives.

We gather the coins into our pockets—shiny quarters, coppery pennies like a river gleam, like lit seeds on an unmowed hayfield, dimes, nickels—our pockets full, we pitch some back and wink at the drive-through attendant who barely believes our kindness to return what we've rightfully found: her mouth open in surprise at our generosity!

Rich as queens, we duck into novelty shops, buy plastic boats, books, in a thrift shop a paper bag of lingerie for one dollar from the fill-a-bag-for-a-buck bin, and parade back to the bank with our boats and our extra change we throw back in, coin by coin. We wish and wish and wish and wish for more.

I wish for a library building, a book castle. I wish for a frosted cookie.

In another town, we are told to wait in the van. Our parents and brother work on a billiards table in the tavern, and we have little toy bears, our snacks, our books, the archives of our imaginations. We leave it all, except our brains. Behind us is a river, we can hear it, smell the tumble of glacial till and damp detritus, but we must navigate a steep slope lush with maples and alders, we have to scramble down to reach the bank, a rock bar where we hop among the boulders looking for ones where our little hips will fit. We settle on some granite lumps from which we can see the other shore—not more than thirty feet across the river, where a more silty-sandy gravel bar juts out in a wide arc just below the field above.

Nothing happens. We sit, we watch the river move around its rocks.

It is as if we are thinking of which book to choose—looking at the opposite shore, not even scanning, really—when we feel the earth begin to vibrate, nearly imperceptible at first, so neither of us speak of it, then noticeable, our bodies humming with the hum and us turning toward each other, then loud like thunder and across the river a cloud of dust and golden moving gods, their hooves and the thrum and the dust we can now taste, its chalky presence, the cloud of these animals' bodies—a herd of wild horses, honey-colored palominos thundering down the bank, the water splashing, their bodies unaware of ours, fixed points, the whole breathing body of horses we are inside of for only a moment, really, before it moves on, and is gone, and we hardly believe it has been there at all except we've both witnessed—been witness to, been one with, the spirit-rich reality of it. The kind of event that, had you been alone, you wouldn't whisper a word of to anyone, for fear it wasn't real, or that sharing would make it less so.

I still think of that as one of the most visceral times of my life, the Wordsworthian experience of that moment, in which all my senses were alive, and I knew nothing.

My mother learns from the tavern manager that a family owns and keeps the land so the horses can live there. Later, I check out a book from the library, read about wild horse herds and how they are in danger in the West, all over America. This herd is an anomaly.

But no amount of information would compete with what I would come to understand as duende, when the wild horses were around me, or the monument my memory has made of it since.

In the early 1990s the rural town where we'd had a Bookmobile replaced the van with a funded, fixed library building. But I still think of the van where first I worked my way through the picture books, young adult novels, moved on to "gardens," eventually went off to college, where the century-old building sat bricked and cavernous and unmovable by wheels and smelled of musty carpet-bag couches and unwatered spider plants.

And later, and now, with digital technology, I know I can access the world—but still when I visit a library, online or in person, I imagine it as a van full of colorful spines, stopping in the closest town, and me inside filling my bag with books I'll then haul in our van around our little corner of the state, the state another library itself, and me a librarian, cataloging plants and coins and wild horses and all the viscera into their little shelves in my mind.

SCAVENGER PANORAMA

I am most myself when poking a dead cow with a stick.

I am twelve years old, and the cow is out in the flood field, its eyes two stuck moons, their orbit interrupted by the water they pulled here, that then pulled them. I'm curious about the interior of the animal—I've already seen a calf birthed dead, the heavy dark blood in dawn fog. When that cow was in labor the men pulled her baby out with chains, hooked to a truck. I heard the moans in the early dark and climbed the fence in my rubber boots, dodging old coils of barbed wire to cross the field to where they worked and she labored. The birth reeked of exhaust and copper. The mother died too. And I've seen a beef carcass—whole, skinned, a marbling of pink and white—in a freezer, the carcass what people in places like ours call *meat*, but the cow had a name. I'm not interested in another pastoral that shows you the honey but not the sting, so I'll tell you, I love the way pus and entrails resemble a universe, and I'll tell you those men were wrong when they used chains to pull a newborn from its mother's pulsing womb, but they knew they'd fucked up when the hemorrhages got so strong that they shot her.

Jane Eyre says, "The shadows are as important as the light," and you know by now that I'm with her, and what's more, I'd elaborate: the stitches are as important as the surface, the source of the scraps or the cut of flank or the knowledge as important as the finished quilt, the cooked meat, the art. I come from a long line of scavengers. Nothing began as beautiful, in the traditional sense, but if you can look at a junked car and see its potential to house a chicken, and the chicken as the origin of a perfect egg, you're going to be okay. Or I think I'm okay. I'm a mother now, zooming back into the snags and pulls of my own memory, wondering what I'll find now that the surge has subsided.

I prod the cow with the stick, wanting it to explode. I'm sad she's dead, but also, I want to know what worlds pulse inside her.

*

Today we think a panorama is the setting to which we slide the control on our phones, then hold steady as we glide from one side of a landscape to the other, the little white arrow remaining in the center of the yellow line until we've reached the end of the view. *Panorama*, from the Greek *pan*, "all," and *horama*, "view." Coined in the late eighteenth century by an Irish painter to describe his Edinburgh settings, panoramas weren't new—they'd been used for over a thousand years in ancient China, as part of handscroll paintings. In the United States, they became widely employed as a tool for showing sweeping views, such as reel renditions of rivers and mountains during the early nineteenth century, and they evolved into uses for various representations in art, media, and science. In film, when we say "panning," we mean the artifice of a camera, as it creates for us a mental sequence, a wide-angle view of a physical space.

*

Many stories contain a flood, and mine is no different.

The land of my coming of age—a broad river valley where typically the Grays River, a tributary of the lower Columbia, winds through lush, silted plains, edged in alders and beyond that, western hemlock, and beyond that, the hills—is covered with water, brown, flowing as if surging over a dike, coming in across the fields, whooshing through the barn. It's biblical. It's apocalyptic. It's environmental disaster. Everywhere the thick scent of earth, the silt and mica and loam and rot, and the quiet of a world gone wild with its own desires: gravity, centrifugal force, and the natural processes of mystery combined with a hydrologic cycle.

Remember that scene in *Where'd you Go, Bernadette?*, when—having razed the earth of its blackberries—the protagonist's whole muddy hillside slides down into the neighbor's house, wrecking the brunch party and depositing a giant Private Property: No Trespassing sign directly into the fancy French doors of the dining room? The neighbor is incredulous in her Seattle way, and Bernadette is responsible for her spite-fueled wreckage. This is my favorite scene of that novel—maybe because of the spite, and maybe because of the flood and how it underscores impermanence and repetition, the flaws of poor planning, without regard to water and soil and the significance of plants and their stabilizing roots.

My family lived (for a while) in an old farmhouse rental situated on fifty acres of floodplain, populated with blackberry bushes and cows and a winding river full of fish and good skipping rocks. Whoever built the house was smart to pour a foundation tall enough that a short flight of steps—four, in my memory—was just right to keep the ground floor a few inches above the highest flood mark, but the house should not have been built in a floodplain at all. Every spring and every fall, when the rains were severe and the forests logged and the ocean tide came up these Columbia tributaries, bringing sea lions and other ocean-dwelling creatures into Seal Slough or Deep River, and right into the valleys, the confluence of factors would converge and flood the entire river basin.

You can look it up, Grays River Valley floods, and your screen will fill with images: the famous covered bridge, surrounded by water and green islands of blackberry vines and fields full of river risen to a blur of beige—the whole of Wahkiakum County a big brown pond. This wasn't an anomaly—it was and is still a reality, recurring as seasonally as a holiday, so that the danger of it we felt that first year gradually became more of a familiar warning, something for which we could prepare: park the cars on the main road's hill; pull anything off the garage, shed, and barn floors; and be ready to drag furniture upstairs if it ever got worse. It never came in the house, except through the bathtub, where the water gurgled through pipes and out the drain, like an alien substance, except familiar, known, filling the white porcelain four inches up, leaving a Cat-in-the-Hat stain and a basin of silt where one might read her fortune in the leavings, like those at the bottom of a strong, well-steeped tea—you can practically see both the map of your life and the delta where rivers braid before the sea.

*

You know that Talking Heads song where he wonders how he got there, to his new life with the "large automobile" and the "beautiful house"?

I feel like that when I wake up every morning. It's true my car is over fifteen years old, but when I turn the key, it starts. Plus, we have one of those bougie jump kits from Costco—where, yes, I buy skorts to wear all summer, because they are great for climbing trees or stopping by the DMV—and no, my closet isn't a walk-in, and it isn't full of linen pants. And my children don't ride ponies, and I haven't been on safari in Africa. But I know when I wake up there will be breakfast, and there will be lunch, later, and dinner—every meal, easy, even though I still feel like a scavenger. A scavenger who soars over a silty, refuse-strewn field, searching for scraps to make something functional and strange.

*

The fields after the floods were full of treasures and ponds of still water, and we'd tromp out like vultures searching for their meals among detritus. Dead animals left days would warm in the sun and bloat so that a stick to the belly could release viscera or a pocket of maggots, their white bodies glistening in their delight at the decay, and a stench that would knock us on our bottoms. We knew what amount of pressure to apply, and when, to rocket an explosion.

Mostly we loved to scavenge gems—an orange buoy we could turn into a barn swing suspended from a long yellow rope, or random items picked up from a neighbor's shed, things they forgot to elevate on shelves. It was like an unintentional swap party of items stolen by nature's reclamation of its own processes. By gravity pulling water out of the sky. By rain.

*

It was this type of rain, on KM Mountain, after the logging and the hill sliding and the mud across State Route 4, that precipitated the closing of my parents' tavern—the latest in a string of failed entrepreneurships. It had just opened that fall, and remained so about a month—my parents gone every night until three o'clock, filling beer glasses and making burgers for the handful of customers, probably not enough to keep it afloat anyway; me kid-sitting my little sister and sometimes staying up until one or two in the morning, wondering when our parents would come home, sometimes going out into the fields to watch the stars and imagine what it would be like when the business made it—new dolls?, Disneyland?, what else did people buy?—and singing *I think we're alone now*, laughing and falling on the ground, collapsing onto the wet earth and thinking of how much freedom we had, but so far away from any mischief we could get into. I was ten and she was seven, and I was the mom that month, again.

When the rains came and the road slid out and stopped the traffic from coming from the I-5 corridor to the beaches—we were just a small dot on a map that no one knew, but my father hoped it would be enough of a dot to sustain a life—and the cars had to go the long way, we knew things were going to get difficult again. But it would get better too. Like water, we remembered where we were before, and before that, and before that. No matter where we were, we were always the shrews coming up from the flood field—always escaping and outrunning, always recreating the home, from the blueprint that rose dripping from our internal architects like instinct.

*

It didn't matter which part of the world or watershed: we knew how to scavenge and stitch. It was in our blood. We grew up visiting Uncle Fred who lives in a house made entirely of parts from the roadside cars he tows in, wears clothes he salvages from abandoned vehicles, and houses his chickens in the nicest automobile on his two acres, an old VW van. He treats his pig with beer from the can. He makes his own carrot juice. He wears pink and red together, and flip-flops in November.

After the tavern closed, my parents got creative again—re-covering the pool tables, selling absorbent cloths in flea markets for cash. I loved watching my father give the demos, the crowd gathering around as he spilled the two-liter of Coca-Cola, soaking it all up with the chamois. Sometimes I'd be in the middle of a math test when they'd pull us from school, *bring your art supplies,* and we'd travel to make our rent money. Driving the Pacific Northwest roads from our rural town, we'd arrive late, park the van, and sleep outside Jewell Towing. My uncle's business sign, flapping above the A-frame bus stop, announced the services at the bottom of his driveway, the gravel disappearing into elderberry, up a hill.

In the morning I wake first, run up the gravel rise, and pound on Uncle Fred's door to tell him we're here. All four feet eleven of him shakes at the threshold of his also-shaky house, like a character from *The Wind in the Willows,* his lip curdled at the mousy girl squishing the moss on his front rocks. "What the hell?" he asks, looking at me, wondering where I've come from.

I envy his chickens, the trees they run through at night, dodging coyotes. Chickens whose heads are the color of grapes.

Fred yells a while until he realizes I'm his niece, and he invites me in, tells me to warm my wet hands by his woodstove. He chuckles a deep dad-laugh when my eyes grow big at all his marijuana, the leaves mottling his trailer in green.

*

To make a panorama, teams of artists used to visit the location, sketch and resketch the sights they wanted to recreate, collaborating to pull together a sweeping scene that emulated the viewing experience if one were immersed in a landscape. Then, gathering the cloth used to make sails, either sail-makers or seamstresses stitched it together, hung as it would be on display, working, as the painters would soon do, from ladders and ropes, eventually cutting it to the right size to be rolled up and then unrolled, creating a visual effect akin to a slow-moving film, or to the sensory impression of being in the landscape depicted. Making a panorama meant teams of athletes and artists of varying accord—not to mention the science of oil paint: pigment suspended in linseed oil, drying at a rate fast enough to maintain quality but slow enough to allow for correction of mistakes. The end result, which so many romantic poets viewed as propaganda (possibly in competition with their verses), appeared smooth and hid errors.

Unlike these early panoramic artists, and unlike those who criticized the art as illusory substitutions for lived experience, I neither care for perfection nor for projecting what *living* is. You can see the seams and ridges, and if you want to sit in your chair and read this instead of driving Route 26—the Sunset Highway—and then 101 and up State Route 4, that's just fine by me. We rummage what we can while we're on this earth, and we map-make and panorama-make in whatever ways we must. Cartography and art are what grownups call it, but I call it scavenging, what the animals do, or what my uncle Fred does, to make his home.

*

When people ask me how I got from there to here, how a person "escapes poverty"—a question that I find irritating, to be honest; I'm not interested in giving life advice because I don't think I'm an expert—I tell them I don't see it as a vertical trajectory. I don't see financial privilege as something I necessarily tried to achieve, though I did want the ground beneath me to be as stable as possible, laced together by the roots of growing things, strong enough in that fibrous rhizome that I didn't become the detritus when the floods came. So I'll tell you: I worked hard but I was also lucky. I went to college on a few scholarships and the scant money I'd saved. Once there I didn't drink lattes or buy any extraneous clothing or go to movies or out to dinner or own a car or take trips overseas. I worked as a custodian all summer, every summer, and I ate frugally and didn't take on debt and didn't throw anything away. I used what I had and kept my bills low and remembered the magic of rivers and hills and the panorama you see when you stand above a river valley as superior to the details of capitalism. I do love the sweeping art of a good painting or architecture, but I don't care for excess. When I visit Europe, stunned I'm there at all, I want to run across the geologic hills and dream about the people and animals who live and lived here, the foliage whose names I know, and those I want to learn. I'm curious about history, know imagination leads us forward and backward, the ebb and flow of memory and curiosity, things I want my children to inherit more than whatever impermanence exists in money. I want them to scavenge their own minds and the world around them and waste nothing except time, wandering about in their own hunger to be animals, to find and to wonder and to remember what shapes them.

Henry David Thoreau published his essay "Walking" in *The Atlantic* in June 1862. He tells us of visiting a panorama of the Rhine.

> It was like a dream of the Middle Ages. I floated down its historic stream in something more than imagination, under bridges built by the Romans, and repaired by later heroes, past cities and castles whose very names were music to my ears, and each of which was the subject of a legend. There were Ehrenbreitstein and Rolandseck and Coblentz, which I knew only in history. They were ruins that interested me chiefly. There seemed to come up from its waters and its vine-clad hills and valleys a hushed

music as of Crusaders departing for the Holy Land. I floated along under the spell of enchantment.

Once I saw the map of the Mississippi River, where it had been before humans rerouted it, and how it was hearkening back to those old lines. These lessons—you cannot control water and if you take away too many trees, the land will become a deluge—were my earliest in ecology, in how it feels in the body. The primal, metal taste of the air when the floods came and went was a hearkening I followed into adolescence.

Later, reading Toni Morrison, I knew she understood.
> "Floods" is the word they use, but in fact it is not flooding; it is remembering. Remembering where it used to be. All water has a perfect memory and is forever trying to get back to where it was. Writers are like that: remembering where we were, that valley we ran through, what the banks were like, the light that was there and the route back to our original place. It is emotional memory—what the nerves and the skin remember as well as how it appeared. And a rush of imagination is our "flooding."

I think of Wahkiakum County and all the watersheds south and west of it, the places that form my internal panorama—not so much visual as visceral—and the ways the water's life changed and shaped the landscape of me. Water and I remember each other.

*

The road was closed at Cathlamet so we could walk the highway during the day, which is what we were doing when our first flood came. We were walking the highway, the fields filling with brown water, and the shrews came up like repentant sinners onto the pavement, a whole flight of shrews running out of the tall grasses, crowding the gray road as the water rose, their small gray bodies frantically migrating to the other side, then turning around and running down the street, toward the tavern. We didn't know the floods would get worse than this high water soon covering the low part in the highway. But our parents took us home, and we drove our cars up the hill, like the neighbors did, and went back to our houses, and waited.

When the water reached the doorstep, we moved our furniture upstairs. I thought about all the animal graves I'd dug by the barn and the things the fields might offer after the water receded. And I thought of how it would be like this for the wild ones too—scavenging their food from the wreckage. A form of foraging, of grazing what was offered by ruin and violence, not so different from the blooming of fruit and flower.

SESTINA FOR FORAGERS

1

Among the things we ate from the forest and ditches, fields and brambles (and rivers beyond) were salmonberries, red hucks, lambs' weed, blackberries (three varieties: Himalayan, evergreen, wild trailing), salmon, stolen jam from restaurant baskets, stolen half-and-half from restaurant baskets, stolen ketchup packets from fast food bins, pumpkins and zucchini wildly overgrown in the gardens, taking over like Europeans, like those who came on boats and planes and clinging and vining and winding their way across the land.

We never called it foraging. Those who eat, by necessity, what's wild and/or found—collage eating—just call it *food*. *Foraging* is a word that rich people use, or people who've chosen to "live off Mother Earth," to embark on a journey the way that people enjoy thrifting—when you shop used clothing stores for the novelty or because it's cool. When you have to shop thrift, there's nothing cool about it. It's just clothes.

I didn't know the word *foraging* until I was in graduate school, when one day, a friend said, "Do you want to go foraging for mushrooms this weekend?"

In my head, I thought "Finding food in the woods? Like, do I want to go back to the most basic of needs?" I believed there was some privilege in simplicity. I wasn't anti-work; it's just that it was emotionally complicated. I could go to the store. I could pay. Also, I didn't know my edible mushrooms then. I knew only my psychedelic.

"No thanks," I said, covering for the tangle inside me.

Later, when I led a public writing workshop themed around plants, noting offhandedly, "Oh, and you can eat it—it's high in vitamin C—" about nettle or mint or rosehips, I don't remember—a participant crooned excitedly, "Oooooh, have you read that book? About foraging? You can find so much that's edible in the wild! We all should be thinking about what we can eat right outside our doorsteps!" and I almost barfed in my mouth. She was right: we should eat what grows for free. And she was right: you can find so much—a constellation of produce is everywhere. But I didn't like her implication in "we should all be thinking"—implying that none of us were thinking about it, that we'd all been raised on Hot Pockets and Pop Tarts, or even that we saw fresh produce as something we could pay a lot of money for at the farmers' market. Fresh produce was always under our noses, if we had the privilege of living where the dirt wasn't covered in concrete. We weren't all living lives of ignorance. It wasn't a mystery. It wasn't exotic.

2

A train of thought is mysterious and many-speared, like a star or sestina.

In the field of poetics, a sestina is all about repurposing, in an incantatory pattern, a repeated set of six end-words, in six sestets and one tercet/envoi, the last containing three lines but all six words, some folded into the middle of the stanza (*like my mind,* I always think to myself when teaching the shape). If you map the pattern, it has a web of six sides.

> *Francis Mayes:* When the sestina was first used in the early twelfth century, the numerology of the sixes probably had a mystical meaning that is lost to us now. What is still fascinating, on inspection of the form, is that each end word is positioned next to every other end word twice in that poem. If we make a hexagon of end words (called ABCDEF) and connect each end word as it touches all the other end words in every stanza, we see that the poem is indeed graphically complete.

Does the sestina work to show you how eating what's in season extends throughout a life, how it departs and returns, like the mythos of memories? Where I live now, the Inland Northwest, the huckleberries are blue and grow wild on the mountain, among the bear grass and the tamarack. The air smells of pollen and lichen and alpine glow. We take our children picking in mid-July and early August, teaching them how to be foragers, to eat what's in front of them, and back home, to make it sweet with flour and sugar and cream. They dream up an unrhymed chant about how the plant grows only in its own soil. It's true: if you try to domesticate it, it dies (*like you,* the children chant, *like you*). A mystery, and a rule. Like foraging. Something we do when we are a little wild inside, not because we want to be, but because it's who we are.

3

My friend, writing a "book of difficult fruit," asks me one day to go with her into the woods on the Olympic Peninsula (north of my childhood watersheds, but climate-wise, fairly congruent). She says, "Let's go berry hunting," and I agree. Walking in the woods—what some call hiking—is one of my favorite things.

"I hate hiking," she tells me, laughing, "but I want to know the plants that produce the fruit." She's honoring every fruit about which she writes, approaching each as ethnography, as lenses into/alongside cultures as she interviews folks, tromps through the woods, builds or watches others build fires with folks who live in rural areas, and pours through history, lore, etymology, medicine, and other ephemera for each chapter and recipe she writes. She's being a star researcher.

I admire and respect her approach. So when she asks me, after our tromp through the woods—during which I note for her the differences between the wild, trailing native blackberries and the two invasive varieties—if she can interview me about my childhood relationship to thimbleberries, I say yes. Unless you're in the woods with me, I don't always talk about my childhood spent eating what I could find in the forest all day, grazing until it was time to go home for dinner.

My friend and I sit in a restaurant when she visits me later to review her progress, to ask about thimbleberries, and the irony of the restaurant booth isn't lost on me (my whole adulthood feels at this point, in some ways, ironic). She's wearing an orange-rust hat she knitted herself. She has domestic skills. I used to have those skills—embroidery, sewing, scratch-made noodles—but now I spend all my time reading other people's writing and not writing my own things. And sometimes I forget to feed the birds.

My friend's questions are her form of foraging for what's edible. I tell her we're all doing this—scavenging and foraging after the floods. But we don't call it that; we just call it being alive. Working. Still, I take cue from her. I begin asking questions, scavenging my past for details, for patterns to repeat.

4

It's worth saying here that the book on foraging is probably excellent. I didn't read it. Ever since Barbara Ehrenreich's appropriative foray into blue collar work in *Nickel and Dimed,* I've balked at the books that make it big in genres for which I'm probably most marketable: poverty, education of people who grow up "living off the land" (practicing some of the earliest and most basic methods of gathering) and "transcend poverty" (eventually making enough money to not have to rely on free lunches or other necessary and humane social services that a nation with enough resources should provide) who were "homeless" (lived in vans, garages, etc.) as children and now live in "regular houses" (i.e., have government-recognized addresses).

I resist these oversimplified descriptors the same way I resist making Inland huckleberries into a marketable commodity, or even a mythic picnic. They're a fruit we eat because it's in season and because we like being in the woods. We leave enough for the bears because we like bears. The stars are what we see from our yard, or on a paddle board at night, not something to chart out in the romanticized wilderness. I know we're lucky to be so close to what's wild, but I also know I come from a people who long ago ran from what wasn't, trying to feel safe, and whole—like Uncle Fred, or my dad, who began foraging for a new life as soon as he set foot on the continent of America, coming across from faraway lands where wild meant this New World.

5

In Uncle Fred's version of reality (which I receive while visiting my uncle in his wild scrap house years later, with my spouse and child), my father was sitting in a bar with some tweakers—brothers of "that woman he was with before your mother"—and Fred came in dressed to the nines in his pinstriped suit he wore to sell used cars in Portland to people who came to the Pacific Northwest for the good life, the way they had from Germany when their mother died, but they ended up in the Northwest where fortunes are as rare as blue sky days. Scratch that. Fortune is the waking bird, the field of notes that float in my uncle's windows where he sleeps and waits for those who call in need of tow. He's foraging his life from the road and stars, piecing it together with rust and salal. His truck is here with its axle orange as a salmonberry. He's seventy, still patching his own roof. His roof is a series of patches, like his body, his beard as gray as that of my father, who Fred purportedly saved. I never know who to believe in these stories. Fred tells stories to my husband and me, while our daughter—age two—sleeps in the car, windows down so if she were awake she could reach out and touch the elderberry forest beyond Fred's chickens and hear the rooster's low grumble as he beckons his hens to a good cache of grubs. My father came with him, Fred tells us, because he was looking for a leg up, and a way to escape the woman.

6

The berries on Highway 26, where Fred lives in his patched-up constellation of a house, grow fat and wild. They're not huckleberries;

they're blackberries, and they glisten on their vines like dark stars working at undoing a heart. I fold my hands into the thorns and leaves for fruit and they come out purple-red. My father is synonymous with a thorned bush; all prickle and stain. He tops my list of those who dig in the forest and swamps: the turkey vulture, the bottom fish, and larger, the nutria, those swamp-rats where the water is lit by reeds and dragonflies. I want these things back now—the fecund rot, the simple arc of season.

7 (Envoi)
Now it's August and the summer of a global pandemic, and all I want is to go back to the most basic of needs. We work our car up the winding road to Mount Spokane, the children—ten and seven—singing and wondering if we can have cobbler for dinner. Or we wander the wild mountains of Montana, eating tart Oregon grapes. For aging is what but returning to the star-shaped sestinas of our internal mythos? I don't believe it; I do believe it. I am afraid of the future. I watch it move like a cloud shadow, across the meadow of wildflowers. My heart-field thrumming with these bright beams. Fire season just beginning.

POVERTY FIRES

> USDA Fire Rating System, **Fire Danger Level: Extreme**
> When the fire danger is "extreme," fires of all types start quickly and burn intensely.... These fires are very difficult to fight and may become very dangerous.

When I was fifteen, I lit a field on fire.

I took water from the river to put it out.

The truth is I wanted to burn something down. The truth is, I *was* down. The truth is, I was burning with hunger, I was drowning in the burn of adolescence, I was just trying to play with matches. The truth is we were poor and we were bored and that was all we had except the barn. We had a horse we had a sky we had a match. The hay in piles, moldy hot inside, hadn't been raked in days. The kind of hay that you can't eat, a horse can't eat—it's no good for hunger.

I had help in the burning. My best friend, whose horses we rode through the floods and the hills, and whose father's car we stole and hid in a ditch a mile from where we stayed the night in an attic house, blue and red lights pulsing outside like a Lite Brite, our wrists pulsing too where we had thought about slashing them. / Slash that. We were okay; we were just filled with hormones. Or maybe we were afraid of our lives and what pains they'd hold later.

We were so okay we jumped in the river. We rode the horses right into the river to put out the fire we'd made in our skins.

*

> **USDA Fire Rating System, Fire Danger Level: Very High**
> When the fire danger is "very high," fires will start easily from most causes. These fires can be difficult to control.

Teens burn down _____ fields a year.

In the HOA where we live, one of the covenants asserts that we should not dump yard waste debris in common areas, "so as to reduce fire hazard," and recently, the association paid to have the Department of Natural Resources evaluate and subsequently clean up the common areas' forest floor, "so as to reduce fire hazard."

People move here to be safe.

Nietzsche says, "Pure vapors are the transformation of sea into fire, the impure ones the transformation of earth to water." And also, "The eternally living fire, Aeon [boy-god of the zodiac], plays, builds, and knocks down: strife, this opposition of different characteristics, directed by justice, may be grasped only as an aesthetic phenomenon. We find here a purely aesthetic view of the world." In a purely aesthetic view of the world, fire is just a bright thing we bring out from the core of ourselves. Or, fire brought the world into existence, transforms all.

Art equals fire equals redemption. The struggle is the fire, is the truth and the way.

I guess I have always been one to stare into the blaze.

When I am forty years old, I consider lighting my perfect life on fire. Then I change my mind.

I understand the impulse for destruction, for ruining things so they might be remade. I understand the desire to make something burn.

Insert here a lot of metaphors involving a mythical phoenix. Insert Heraclitus, Plato, Shiva. Insert philosophy, or at least its impulse. Reason always takes everything too far from the glow.

*

> *USDA Fire Rating System,* **Fire Danger Level: High**
> When the fire danger is "high," fires can start easily ... small fuels (such as grasses and needles) will ignite readily. Fires can become serious ... unless they are put out while they are still small.

In the western United States, we now have three seasons: snow/rain, spring, and fire.

Every year the fires burn down another place I love. Two years ago, on one of my favorite trails, I sat and watched from a ridge as helicopters dropped chemicals on a bright orange glow on one of my other favorite trails across the river valley. It was all underbrush and delicate shade plants; now it's all thistle and charred trunks. I still walk it, but for a while, I had to watch out so as not to slip in the after-sludge, a thick black muck that overtook the ground, like the ash after a volcanic eruption.

As I write this, the redwoods in California have gone up in a blaze—thousands of years of pith mapping water, ringed and exquisite, gone. Homes for all those birds and insects and squirrels. Homes of humans too. At the White House, Melania Trump removed Jackie Kennedy's crab apples and replaced all the color with white flowers. In my rage, I want to light her house on fire. It reminds me of Rick Barot, in "The Garden."

> When I read about the garden
> designed to bloom only white flowers,
> I think about the Spanish friar who saw one
> of my grandmothers, two hundred years
> removed, and fucked her. (lines 1–5)

His poem moves into colonization, language origins, and snow, and I think, these things are not unrelated: whitewashing, climate change, the world ending. I think: it doesn't matter who you are, the end of the world is coming for you. I think: yes, I'm lucky, but for how long? And who is suffering the stench of smoke right now, the lack of clean water? And where are we on the rating system? Can we put out the spark while it's still small?

Will there be any hope for a rebirth from the ashes? I think of foxgloves or fireweed populating a hillside where logging or wildfires razed the earth. I think of the ash fields surrounding Mount Saint Helens, or the Willapa Hills, the stretches of spaces where Weyerhaeuser took out the hemlocks, the whole mountain stained purple with the beautiful wound. How I ate it when I was younger. How that wound sustained me.

*

USDA Fire Rating System, **Fire Danger Level: Moderate**

When the fire danger is "moderate" it means that fires can start from most accidental causes.

A BRIEF CATALOG OF FLAMMABLE ITEMS
& THE PEOPLE WHO BURNED THEM

Flammable Item	Father	Brother	Maya	Faulkner
arrows, homemade for homemade bows		✓	✓	
barns				✓
barn hay		✓	✓	✓
black beetle, trapped under a mason jar with dry straw and twig		✓		
books (banned)				
bra, hand-me-down, in resentment			✓	
brush	✓	✓	✓	
burn barrel, full of regular household trash	✓		✓	
candles (for which we melted old crayons down and rolled twine in wax)		✓	✓	
fields			✓	
joints, rolled	✓			
love letters				
mint, testing to see if it really smelled like marijuana, as the DARE officer said it would, when you think to yourself, "this program is what a school should instate if it wants teens to be very curious about doing drugs, to the point where they try them if they haven't yet"			✓	
notes we passed in class that might incriminate our parents for the ways they broke the law			✓	
old clothes we hated		✓	✓	
pipe, full of tobacco or marijuana	✓			
small piles in the forest, meant for roasting hot dogs or for burning our shame		✓		
wood stove tinder (morning, water boiling, for making oatmeal OR evening, water boiling, for making a bath)	✓	✓	✓	

I learned the ways of flint and stick and coal and blue-orange glow from men with lighters and kerosene, in burn barrels and forests and woodstoves and schools. I learned something lit can spread and scorch an earth or arm or house or barn.

Ray Bradbury: "It was a pleasure to burn. It was a special pleasure to see things eaten, to see things blackened and changed."

Henry David Thoreau: "Cultivate poverty like a garden herb, like sage."

*

> USDA Fire Rating System, **Fire Danger Level: Low**
> When the fire danger is "low" it means that fuels do not ignite easily from small embers, but a more intense heat source, such as lightning, may start fires in duff or dry rotten wood.

My son loves to make a small pyramid of kindling in our backyard pit, under the spruces and pines. We let him do this until the end of June, when either the county or our own common sense says it's too dry. We let him fill it with newspaper and touch the green-headed match to the edge of a picture, and we watch his eyes mirror the dance of the flame.

We live in a neighborhood north of a city, where people water their lawns to keep them lush—ours mossy and brown-green but still a buffer to potential wildfire—and we fill the bird baths so the doe can drink and nurse her fawns. When lightning comes we watch it out the large front window, ready to call the fire department if the dry inland pines are struck and blaze. We're not likely to simmer to the ground or end in embers. Some Augusts the air here is so full of smoke we can't go outside. Some Septembers, school is delayed because they can't ventilate enough to allow children into classrooms. Some summers the fires are so close we know we could be the next California, the next Australia. We cry for California, Colorado, Australia, everywhere being destroyed.

I worry when I feel the wick still flickering inside me. I worry when I flick the match against the box. I worry how complicit I am, right down to my bones. I worry about metaphor and pleasure, about driving across town. I worry the way a mom worries, or a teenager who knows she's the root of trouble, jumping from the highest rafter in the barn, landing on hay she knows she'd burn if she grew too angry. I get in my car again, dragging my fossil fuels down the road. I worry the whole freeway from here to wherever I'm going in my fossil fuel car, like lighting the field on fire, over and over again.

COMPLETE THE SENTENCE

My seven-year-old son comes home with a worksheet from this week's spelling practice.

> **Directions:** Look at this week's spelling words in the box below. Then, write a spelling word to complete each sentence.

    roast   going   both   float   grow
    loaf   cold   bowl   throw soap

The choices begin like this:

1. Do you think the pen will sink or _____?
2. We baked a fresh _____ for dinner.

We baked a fresh *bowl* for dinner?, I wonder. Do you think the pen will sink or *grow*? Do you think a pen will sink or *throw*? Sure. This could be a very delightful exercise, I think to myself.

My ten-year-old daughter explains that you just guess what they want you to put. You just try to think of what your teacher would do, she says, and you do that.

Her brother has gotten two wrong. They are numbers four and eight, which he has transposed:

Mom will make her pot cold   on Saturday.
The wind made the weather feel roast .

Yes, I think. Mom will make her pot cold on Saturday. It has been warm from tea all week; on Saturday, she will wash it and put it away. Or maybe her cold outdoor pots have been full of ferns she needs to move indoors. Warm wind does make the weather feel quite roast.

"What's roast?" my son asks.

It means hot, we explain. Or, I say, pot roast is a cooked meat, in a crock pot.

"Ew," says my son. He does not eat meat, and perhaps not uncoincidentally never has seen nor heard of pot roast. I have never made it. I have not made it on Saturday, and I have not made it any other day. I see the problem. This question had no cultural context for him, as it would have no cultural context for any child who had never heard of a pot roast, or who doesn't use shampoo and soap when they shower, or who doesn't bake a fresh loaf for dinner, or who doesn't eat a bowl of cereal before school. This test has quite a bit of cognitive dissonance for those children, I explain to mine. It's a problem of cultural literacy.

We know, says the ten-year-old. When you were a child, this would have been confusing to you.

No, I say, I read, and I understood prediction, so I imagined what they would want, like you do, and then I would answer based on context clues.

"Like on the SAT," says my children's father.

"What's the SAT," says our daughter.

"It's a test, not for your mom."

"But I did okay."

"Yes, she did okay, because she could guess. She did a little better than me," he says. "But she should have done a lot better—she's smarter. It's just that the test was made more for me. I had taken Latin."

"What are the questions like?" our daughter asks.

Her father thinks. "Like this: **A branch is to a tree, as a chair is to a . . .**"

Me: "Oh! I know this one! As a child, I would have thought (a) *barn*, or (b) *furniture store*. But the answer is (c) *living room!*"

"No," says my ten-year-old. "It's *table*."

My husband gives me the pity look, or maybe it's disapproval. "Yeah, table. It's table, Maya."

"Oh," I say, quietly. I feel a weird shame. "I thought it was living room. I thought that would be right. I didn't even think of table."

"See," my husband says to our children. "The test wasn't made for your mom."

"But," I say, proudly, "our family would do very well on *Family Feud*. We know how to help each other," I say. "We know how to work together."

"No," says my husband. "You're not the demographic for that, either. You have no idea how to imagine America."

*

My friend Ellie tells me later, "It's dining set." She was raised outside of Boston.

*

I look at a practice SAT question from the internet. It goes like this:

> **Directions:** In the following question, a related pair of words or phrases is followed by five pairs of words or phrases. Choose the pair that best expresses a relationship similar to that in the original pair.

MEDICINE : ILLNESS ::

    hunger : thirst
    etiquette : discipline
    law : anarchy
    love : treason
    stimulant : sensitivity

I hold two degrees from reputable institutions of higher learning. Both of my degrees are related to the English language and its usage. I do not initially see the clear answer to this practice question. I reason it out: medicine *heals* illness. Which of the other word pairs is about *healing*?

Hunger heals thirst?

When I was gone a long time from the house—in the forest, along the river, or hauling hay from a neighbor's field—and getting hungry, I had a few tactics: Drink more water. Eat what's edible in season: salmonberries, thimbleberries, blackberries, huckleberries. If nothing's in season, chew a grass stem, drink the nectar from a clover. Do a bee dance. Pretend it's not raining. Huddle in the barn and write a story in your head: we're children who somehow lost their parents! (Our library books taught us the rules of YA lit.) Outside, the staccato pings on the barn's roof the same rhythm as flitting trout in the shallows. Walk in the rain and pretend you're a fish. The air carries the waft of cow manure off the field fog. My hems mud-soaked and frayed. I could strip off these clothes and hang them by the woodstove, heat water, drink more tea. We usually had eggs from the chickens and salmon from the river. If we didn't, we would again soon. Walk in the rain and pretend you're a fish. Go in the house and get dry clothes. What was I thirsty for? What hunger could possibly heal it?

Etiquette heals discipline?

I'd read of etiquette in books. I knew curtsy, please, thank you, cross your legs, fold your hands in your lap, don't interrupt your father. It involved Don't Tell Your Classmates Your Father Smokes Pot, involved Be Quiet When He Speaks. It involved a lot of being quiet. At my request—my begging, actually, because

I'd heard of but never experienced church—my mother took me to mass once when I was five. It involved a lot of kneeling and very beautiful stained-glass windows and a man who droned and people in robes who sang. It involved leaving before the priest could ask my mother where she'd been for the last seven years. Discipline was making the bed. Staying in the van while our parents re-covered billiards tables in taverns in strange towns. Completing the chore list. Saturday mornings we had to do all of it before we could scamper into the woods, field, barn. Before we could go down to the river, the grasses bending like penitents, the religion of currents, the gray sky that smelled of rain. No manner of pleasing or thanking or curtsying got you out of chopping kindling or making bread. Don't share the bread; we have only so much bread. What was the difference between discipline and etiquette? Both felt like something you did because someone expected it.

Law heals anarchy?

I'm fourteen.

I need a ride home from sportspracticeafterschoolclubASBFuture-BusinessLeadersofAmerica. I want to go to college, and I do all the things I think they'd recommend. Except for music, for which you must rent an unaffordable instrument. All the things happen after school. I need a ride home. My mother says "I can't pick you up. Your father can't pick you up. You'll have to ask a friend." Asking a friend is not possible; no one lives where we live. Don't ask the coach/advisor/teacher. They can't know too much or they'll get nosy. I decide it's best to quit the sportafterschoolclubASBFBLA.

My father was more than once arrested and spent a night in jail for driving under the influence. My mother tells the story like this: My father was driving home from work. He had had maybe one beer (this is an understatement, and she also leaves out the fact of the one open in the middle console). Behind him, a cop pulled up too close, shining his lights in my father's rearview mirror. Unable to see, my father swerved. Pulled over, he refused to take a Breathalyzer. (Who knows whose mouth has been on that thing? my mother says, the same way she says, We don't eat that garbage, referring to foodbankwhitebread foodbankVelveetacheese foodbankdonuts foodbankFranzcookies.) They threw him in jail! Can you believe that? For shining *their* lights in *his* mirror! She slams the rolling pin against the dough. The bread dents and slowly reforms, with only a small incline in its yeasty surface. A little rolling pin to the dough doesn't stop it. It knows how to bounce back.

After a night in jail, my father, nervous but undeterred, cuts back on drinking, grows more marijuana under the bright light in the closet. He keeps railing against the establishment.

He never completed his court requirements after the last time he was caught. Complete the sentence: He <u>drives</u> now without a <u>license</u>.

Complete the sentence: My father, made of <u>anarchy</u>, was never healed by <u>law</u>.

I know this, *law heals anarchy,* is the answer they want; I know, too, it isn't true.

*

My high school—I changed high schools three times; I mean my last one, the one I attended the latter half of junior and the end of senior year—did not have advanced or college placement courses—there were only seventeen of us in my class. So I learned whatever the majority of my peers needed to learn. I was often academically bored (as so many are in public schools) and serving as an unofficial TA, helping classmates meet standards, though there were plenty of cultural things they understood that I did not—things cable television taught them or participating in normative American traditions taught them. For instance, my peers knew they'd attend college, or community college, or go straight to working in the forest, cutting down trees with their fathers. And they seemed to know the steps to achieving these outcomes. I remember asking my math teacher what skills we hadn't covered that might be on the SAT. His brow furrowed and his neck turned red. I asked if I could skip the next test and just read ahead because next week I'd be taking the SAT. I wanted to be sure I was at least aware of the functions, even if I didn't know how to do them. If I knew the formulas, maybe I'd perform okay. He let me skip class and sit in the cafeteria in order to read ahead in the textbook. He said he was sorry he didn't have time to teach me himself. He said good luck. He said don't worry about the verbal; you're going to do great.

I had to save a long time at my Sunday and two-evenings-a-week job as a courtesy clerk to afford the SAT. After taxes, my $4.90 an hour shrunk to about $3 an hour, so my paychecks for the ten hours of work I managed after school, studying, and extracurriculars—some because I enjoyed them, some to get into college—totaled about $63 for two weeks' work, before deductions for the groceries I brought home. Sometimes my mother called and said Maya can you bring home milk (-$4.99), Maya can you just pick up some green peppers (-$2.50), Maya just some flour (-$3.29). My paychecks were often less than $50. It was 1996, and I was determinedly saving for college, but I also had bills: running shoes, sports bra, work shirt, college applications, senior pictures, prom dress, SAT. I was able to catch a ride to take the test (an hour away) with a friend who had a crush on me. I didn't study or take a prep class—I didn't know people did that. I took the test only once. My score: 640 verbal, 630 math. Good enough to get into college. I crossed my fingers and applied to the one university I most wanted to attend.

*

I call in my ten-year-old to check my work. I show her the original question.

She scans, then says, "Medicine fixes illness. One of these fixes the other. What's *anarchy*?"

"Chaos," I say, "or lawlessness."

"Okay," she says, quickly, "that's the answer."

How can she be so sure?

*

Between haying, babysitting, hoarding my $5 a year birthday money from my grandmother in Iowa, and the job at the grocery store, I managed to save $2,000 for college. I applied for scholarships and filled out the FAFSA, and I was lucky in that my parents made so little money that I qualified for the lowest-interest loans. That first year, I didn't take the loans. I was terrified of debt, terrified it would bring me back.

*

SAT / Verbal / Analogy

Directions: In the following question, a related pair of words or phrases is followed by five pairs of words or phrases. Choose the pair that best expresses a relationship similar to that in the original pair.

Maya : College ::

daughter : certainty
mud : hem
Maya's Dad : DUI
darn : sock
casual debt : middle class

*

It takes very little research to uncover the ways that the SAT—and other tests like it—privilege specific socioeconomic groups, races, and genders.

America is systemically set up for white people, even rural white people, to overcome many obstacles. So the SAT, despite being a cultural literacy to which I did not have access, was a cultural literacy for which I could nevertheless determine the route to success, even with a library open only a few days a week (and to which I didn't even have to ride my bicycle—my mother was a huge fan of libraries; not all rural youth have this advantage). And, despite my limited resources, I was allowed to pursue independent study—my teacher sent me to the empty cafeteria with my textbook and trusted that's what I'd be doing, unsupervised, though it was technically his credibility on the line for leaving me unsupervised.

I'm curious: How many people, raised in working-class rural America, understand enough about the process to succeed on SATs, obtain a BA, and then go on to earn an advanced degree? And what are these people's scores like?

*

"We don't want to hear about your SAT scores, we want to hear about your childhood," says my friend Laura, when I ask her to talk about the SAT prep course she took in high school. But I'm stubborn (one of the qualities that helped me succeed), so I ask her son—a student reference librarian at Reed College, who scored an almost-perfect 1560 on the SAT—to help me figure out how to research the narrative experiences of those who grew up in rural poverty, did not study for the SAT, and somehow went on to achieve graduate degrees. He says, smiling benevolently, "You mean you?"

I tell him I mean that demographic, and is it easiest to find this information through a database, or should I just do a Twitter poll?

He says, "Yeah, you'll want to create an algorithm and do a search."

I know what an algorithm is, but I have no idea how to make one, so I watch YouTube videos on algorithm basics for about nine minutes and feel like I can make a solid algorithm flow chart of what I want, but I'm not sure how to transfer that into code and then apply to Twitter.

"An algorithm is just a set of directions," says my ten-year-old, walking through the room. "That's what my library teacher tells us." She pauses to watch her lava lamp. "So just write a series of directions."

"Yeah," says the seven-year-old, smugly. "An algorithm is easy. Anyone can write one."

Here's a set of directions: Find me some stories of people with those criteria.

But neither the genius twenty-year-old nor the genius ten-year-old (nor the genius seven-year-old) give me any instructions on how to code an algorithm and apply it to research, so I decide, instead, to listen to Laura.

*

When students register with the College Board to take the SAT, they complete a questionnaire of forty-three items that include things like race/ethnicity, parental education, combined family income, high school courses taken, grades, extracurricular interests, intended major. When I was registering for the SAT, we would have completed this questionnaire on paper. I don't remember what I wrote then, but I can imagine it went something like this:

Combined family income: $25,000
Intended major: Education.

Parental education: Mother: BA [obtained when I was in elementary school]; Father: No HS diploma.

*

My father dropped out of school during his sophomore year, shortly after his father remarried. His mother was dead of cancer and his stepmother, Ursula (truly her name!), didn't like her stepson. This is how the story is told: a small crime happened in the neighborhood, and Ursula volunteered my father as a suspect. I don't know if he committed the crime or not; I know he was blamed. This incident was a self-fulfilling prophecy. My father ran away from home, dropped out of school, and joined up with some "bad" kids. They scavenged things to pawn or to eat; they pilfered turkeys from poultry farms, stole scrap metal to sell for profit. My father was good at geometry and math in general; he was able to calculate how to do well on the streets and how to avoid the law, until he wasn't. He ended up in a boys' detention center for juvenile delinquents. Like something out of a novel, they beat the boys and locked them in dark holes for solitary confinement for up to three days at a time, without food or human contact. My father says they lowered water down to him. When the accreditation agency came to review the program, the boys were given strict instructions on what to say; my father estimated the chances he'd be beaten for telling the truth versus the chances he'd be released. When his turn came, my father decided to report the actual events of his incarceration: that he was mistreated, that he was threatened, coached, coerced, and poorly fed. The visitors got him out, the program was put on probation, and my father speculates, soon thereafter closed.

My father hedged his bets, but he also understood probability and the formulaic likelihood that he'd be disbelieved and later beaten— he understood telling the truth was his best shot.

*

Here is an example of an SAT Math question:

> Roberto is an insurance agent who sells two types of policies: a $50,000 policy and a $100,000 policy. Last month, his goal was to sell at least 57 insurance policies. While he did not meet his goal, the total value of the policies he sold was over $3,000,000. Which of the following systems of inequalities describes x, the possible number of $50,000 policies, and y, the possible number of $100,000 policies, that Roberto sold last month?
>
> A) $x + y < 57$
> $50,000x + 100,000y < 3,000,000$
>
> B) $x + y > 57$
> $50,000x + 100,000y > 3,000,000$
>
> C) $x + y < 57$
> $50,000x + 100,000y > 3,000,000$
>
> D) $x + y > 57$
> $50,000x + 100,000y < 3,000,000$

My daughter looks at this problem and immediately says it's C.

I look at this problem and agree it's C, but I also imagine how Roberto had trouble selling insurance in America.

And what are these policies he's selling for $50K and $100K? And what's his take of the $3 million? And does Roberto have a family? Why does he sell insurance?

When I was taking the SAT, I would have wondered: Who in the world buys those policies, anyway? Who has enough money to purchase insurance?

I sit and imagine the many ways to complete a life.

*

Directions: Look at the word boxes below. Decide which word box best fits your childhood. Then choose a set of sentences that work for your word box.

OR come up with a set of sentences for your childhood. Then redact the words and create a word box for your childhood. Finally, write a word to complete each sentence below.

IF these directions don't work, invent your own. Complete a set of sentences that work with them.

barn	teach	rain		grass stem	nectar	
salmon	write	wood stove		fish		galvanized cabasa

sink	swim		stick of gum	milk	fish
tub	water heater		path	adult	doghouse

In adult life, do you think Maya will _____ or _____?
We used to bathe in the _____ , warming our water on the _____.

RAISED BY FERNS

We caught a fresh _____ for dinner.
Walk in the _____ and pretend you're a _____.
If you're hungry, chew a _____, drink _____.
The staccato pings on the ____ roof.

TWO

MASLOW'S HIERARCHY OF NEEDS

I got the moon in my forehead on a lukewarm day in late fall, 1983, in La Pine, Oregon.

My brother and I had been throwing a plate back and forth, pretending it was a frisbee, over the dormant stalks of peas and pole beans—or tomatoes and beet leaves?—that was our mother's garden. The plate, a thick polystyrene, spun like Saturn, or like our dangerous take on the merry-go-round, the kind where once you're on, you don't leap off until the many children pushing, wearing ruts around you like satellites in orbit, stop, and you can finally release your sticky grip on the hand-warm metal.

It was a day like that—two poverty kids making do. Who needed store-bought discs? We loved improvising; we were trained to Pollyanna everything.

Our mother poked her head outside and said, "If you don't stop throwing that plate, someone's getting hurt." She didn't mean she'd beat us—did she? we barely wondered, not like when Dad threatened to pull the car over "if those kids don't shut up," and then, when we didn't shut up, actually *did* pull the car over, yanked his belt from his waist—I don't think she did. But when she went inside, my brother gave the disc one last whip and I saw it, coming toward me, a harbinger of the unfortunate complications of the rest of my life. I could see that it was about to happen. I ducked, it ducked. And we had to have Bob and Jean across the street drive me to Bend, an hour away, to the emergency room. I got to lie down in the back of the car all the way there. I had bled all down my front and my jeans so they had to strip me down to my underwear and tank top and wrap me in a blanket so I didn't get blood all over the back seat of Bob's car. The blood was warm and sticky and thick, and at first when I fell over and then put my fingers to the moon-shaped, now-jagged wound of a bumpy dinner plate, I thought perhaps a natural water spring was gushing over me, something must have spilled, there was so much water, and I thought of the sea, and swimming, and almost drowning. Or maybe the drowning was later. Primal memories are like this: the wolf pack of them swimming together in the mind. Memory, that tiny jellyfish, plinking through.

That was how I came to have the moon there, forevermore, thirteen stitches. The kind doctor—who I remember as attractive, though that doesn't seem right, as I was four—blew into a rubber glove and let me hold it while he gently pulled out bits of plate. And afterward, ice cream and a car ride during which I could lie down and watch the windows darken and fill with stars, my stars, the constellation that spilled out when the moon was cut open. It was better than a birthday. I would have hurt myself again.

*

Self-Actualization: Is it marrying poems?

"If you love Poems so much," says Beadlebaum, the bully in a Sabrina Orah Mark short story, "why don't you marry Poems?"

"I did marry Poems," says the narrator. "We've been married for years."

***Esteem*:** Talking to a rock, talking to a tree, having the tree talk back. Treetalk. Rocktalk. Talk back might be the bark, or the beetles, or the other calligraphic needs of the forest, scrawling across the surface of the vascular cambium. See the layers of a woody stem, outside to inside, in mature state: bark/periderm, vascular cambium, wood/sapwood/heartwood, pith. Who knows which layer is the self? Which is the self in or out of love?

***Love*:** _____. Does anyone know? Lorca: "Duende is a struggle, not a concept." Love's a struggle too.

***Safety*:** Children, living, after traumatic birth. Children tucked into a tree fort. Children in the nook of their mother, herself a nook, a tree, a calligraphy that spells Here I Am.

***Physiological*:** Stones, river, clouds, dirt, trees, sky, mountains, books, running. Running river, river stone, stone mountains, mountains of dirt, dirt full of trees, tree-full sky. A sky, slate-smooth, the color of stone. Or ocean.

*

I'm in the shower, and my son, age seven, stands outside of it, telling me how he misses his Montessori preschool, where, he says, "You were allowed to learn what you wanted to learn, and the whole school—or even class—didn't have to be doing the same things at the same time." He contrasts it to our neighborhood school he attends now.

"I'm sorry bud," I tell him. I lather my hair. "We miss it too. It was wonderful! But it ended at kindergarten. We kept you there last year—when you could have gone to public school for free—even though it was expensive!" It was comparable to what we would have paid for childcare in preschool, but, we thought, a better investment. That last year, we opted to stay to complete the Montessori three-year cycle. He was finally thriving socially, and we didn't want to disrupt his excitement about learning. *Thriving socially* was something I learned in a textbook my junior year of college. I kept it in the parent wordbank. It wasn't treetalk, but then, maybe it was, the ways their roots rhizome into an underground communication system with the mycelium network.

"How expensive?" he wants to know. "Wait! Let me guess." He begins at "One Thousand a Month!" I tell him "a little lower," and after several attempts, he gets it: $800 a month, for all day. "How much does my new school cost?" he asks. The scent of coconut steams off my neck, clashing with the riverstone walls of the shower. I know the difference, though: these walls are smoother to the touch; a creek bed is bumpy like something alive.

"It's free," I tell him, but then I realize my mistake. "Well, not free. We pay through property taxes." The hot water feels so good on my back—I've returned from my Saturday run in the snow and rain, another kind of goodfeel.

"What about kids whose families don't own a home?" he asks. I can tell he's into this conversation—ready for its complexities. He understands percentages, so I say, "Well, if they pay rent, whoever owns the place they live pays a percent through their taxes. So those families pay . . . just indirectly."

"Less?" he asks.

"It's difficult to calculate. I like to hope so. If you have less money, you should pay less."

"What about if you don't have a house at all?" he asks. "Then is it free?"

"Well, in that case, I mean . . . you don't go to school sometimes. Or if you do, you don't pay. But it's hard to go to school if you don't have a house." I lather my hair, hurrying. The privilegeguilt is seeping out of the split ends.

"Like you, when you were a kid?" he asks.

"No, we usually had a place to stay," I say. "I only didn't go to school in kindergarten because . . . we were staying . . ."

"In a van down by the river?" he asks, but he's really finishing a formula. I almost laugh to hear him say this. I've never described it that way, but clearly, he has heard this depiction of off-grid living. He's heard me talk about "jumping in the river" instead of having a bath or shower. Jumping in the river, but not with soap. Soap would hurt the fish. We had no lotion on our bodies—only aloe vera (from the plant, not the bottle), and sweat, and the forest.

"Well, we were crashing in our friend Larry's rental, in between renters. So I went to school for a week. But we couldn't stay there, so my parents pulled me out of school."

"And you lived in the van?"

"And we lived in the van." I wash off my soap lather and turn off the shower, the hot steam curling around me. Thinking of water conservation, I don't shave. I remember being a child his age, bathing this time of year in our galvanized basin, the water we'd melt sometimes from roof-icicles and heat on the woodstove in winter, because the pump was frozen or the water we were able to pull from the ground had to be for drinking.

I can hear his brain-wheels. "So did your parents not pay for school?" He's thinking about it: we paid for him to attend Montessori School, whereas I didn't attend kindergarten longer than a week. Then, "And you didn't get to do the maths you wanted, like I did before." I step out, wrapped in my towel. He looks at me with his large, sympathetic eyes. His empathy-eyes.

Not like his school now, he infers, where his math skills—the ability to do fractions and division when we enrolled him last year, in first grade—lay buried under his "lack" of reading fluency. Said the teacher, "His math skills are fine, so we'll just keep him with his peers so he can build confidence. . . . We don't want him to feel like he's different." He's quiet and doesn't say much in school so soon tests into LAP—the Learning Assistance Program—where for several days a week he uses electronics to help him develop his reading skills. In math, he's (re-)learning subtraction. He tells us math is dull and that he hates reading. His favorite subjects now are PE and recess, where he is allowed to move his body. He often complains of boredom but knows better than to complain too much. He knows he's lucky to go to school at all. He knows how hard I work to give him his life, because we don't keep it a secret. I wonder if we do any damage by our blunt honesty about these things. I wonder if we're doing him a disservice sending him to his current school, or not advocating harder for advanced math, a subject in which he has not learned anything new in over a year and a half, since arriving there. I wonder how often my parents asked these questions—did they have any time at all to consider them, while they were trying every day to figure out things like where we'd stay and what our next meals might be?

*

In 1943, after spending time with the Blackfoot—Siksika—people, scholar and psychologist Abraham Maslow introduced, in his paper "A Theory of Human Motivation," a hierarchy of basic and psychological needs that he believed must be met before a human could approach needs of self-fulfillment. That Maslow borrowed the paradigm from Indigenous people is rarely brought up.

Since then, many schools and workplaces have used the pyramid—depicted with slight differences according to the source—to establish a tool for pedagogy or philosophy of workplace management to increase productivity and balance.

Across depictions, the pyramid is built upward from basic needs such as food and shelter, to psychological or love/belonging needs such as friendship and family, and feelings of worth, to esteem and self-fulfillment, creative activities, reaching problem-solving potential, etcetera. Some place things like sex and employment security at the bottom, and others consider those higher up. Here are two contemporary models, the one on top from the popular "Dummies' Guide To" series, and the other from an unattributed Pinterest site.

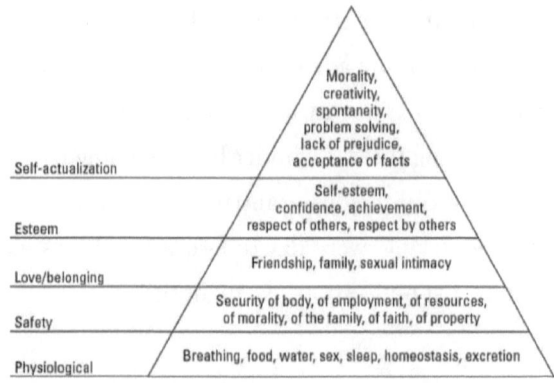

Maslow's Hierarchy of Needs, from "Dummies Guide To..."

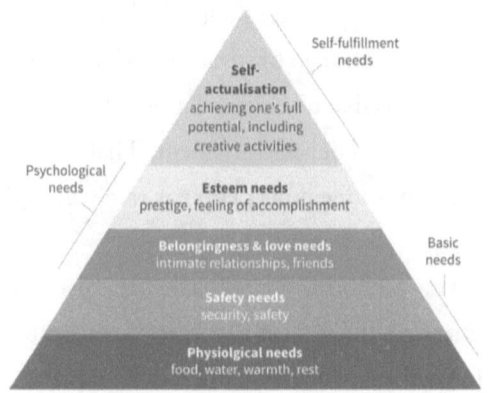

Maslow's Hierarchy of Needs, Pinterest

Depending on your personal needs, positionality, history of privilege and access, and what you've ever personally lacked, you might rearrange these. Depending on your personal views of research and source material, you might find better graphs. I like using those that most people will find from a quick internet search, because most people have not had the access, tools, and education to seek other sources. I like thinking a mother at home, or an artist in her studio, or a person preparing a lecture on Acceptance of Facts or Poetics of Problem-Solving will all be able to find it if they have 0.45 second and a high-speed internet browser or phone.

Anyone who says time is their most-treasured resource knows what I mean. As a mother and full-time professor and part-time writer, I know what I mean.

*

Wrote Aristotle: "All paid work absorbs and degrades the mind." But Aristotle lived in a different time, and now paid work might make it possible for the mind to exist. Wrote Art Alexakis, lyricist of the punk rock band Everclear, "I hate those people who love to tell you / money is the root of all that kills." He points out that anyone who thinks this has never experienced poverty nor welfare, has never had to live through the shame of a holiday with less-than. It's possible Art also lived in another time—he's seventeen years my senior, from California—but maybe he gets it: being poor can make you feel so worthless in a capitalist society that you don't have a lot of emotional energy left for the mind's development. When it comes to Maslow's Hierarchy, I'm probably somewhere between Aristotle and Art. I'm in the woods with the moon. I'm with the whales.

But where are you *from*? People often ask.

My friend Laura says it's important for people to understand my chronology. She says, "You moved so much, people will get confused." She says, "Tell your home story, straight through, at least once."

I don't understand my home story, really—I consider myself to be mostly of the Lower Columbia Basin Watershed, though I don't really believe in that name—but I've practiced saying "near Astoria" for when I must answer that. And when I must say my home story, I might say it like this:

> I was born in 1979, right at the height of the gas crisis/low of the shortage, in a gas station on the Oregon Coast, where I lived for two years, my basic needs met. (My uncle Fred and my father and one of their friends, during this time, also purchased two acres in the forest in Jewell, Oregon, on Highway 26. My uncle Fred still owns it—under some point of contention, since my father never "got his share back." Uncle Fred's house is made of salvaged wood and old car parts, and his chickens live in a VW bus, and his wardrobe is comprised of clothing he pulls from junked vehicles, and he gives his three-hundred-pound pig a can of beer most afternoons. He also has had a fabulous marijuana garden as long as I've known him. But Uncle Fred and his Plexiglas and old house and his pink shirt with red shorts and his beer-guzzling pig are another story.) My needs were met. Or I don't remember. I'm still alive, so let's assume that after the long labor and the gibbous moon and the baptism in the creek that meets the sea, and the smell of gasoline and breast milk together forming an olfactory wonder, my first year was lovely. Or it wasn't. I don't know.

When I was about a year old, the gas station, Barry's by the Sea, went—after a brief stint at self-employment, small-biz success—completely out of business. My parents sold the building to "the woman up the hill," who, believing it always an eyesore, immediately burned it to the ground. I was two when we moved to central Oregon, where my father, and his friend, homeless Joe, opened a gas station and tow business. That lasted a few months. I'm not sure why it didn't succeed, but I hear my father say something about Joe and his friends stealing all the money and driving off, and they couldn't make the bills. My parents were buying, meanwhile, through monthly payments to the owner, an acre of land—scrubby sage, ponderosas, sand, red rock. We lived in the trailer (yes, trailer with wheels, no, not by the river, not this time) until the gas station went out of business, then they sold the trailer to pay for groceries, and we moved into the garage, a free-standing, uninsulated outbuilding with a woodstove, where we lived for the rest of that year—the winter turned cold and we covered the walls with my father's serapes—wool blankets and shawls he brought back from Mexico so long ago and had made the move with us.

My sister was born there, blue as the faraway ocean, and I slept through the birth in my cot, waking in the morning cold and furious that I didn't get to catch her. I was three. My brother was six. I don't know if we lived in the garage the whole time or if we lived in the bus or van.

I also don't know what my parents did during this time for money. Sure, my father sold the chamois at flea markets, off and on during my childhood, so I imagine he must have relied on that and found odd jobs and fixed cars and bartered things from other things, as my father does.

Eventually, we left—we drove away, stopping in Manzanita for a bit, crashing at the empty rental house of our friend Larry (uncle of Sarah Jo, of Sarah Jo's caramels), during a one- or two-week window when I was enrolled and then quickly pulled from kindergarten, because the house found renters, so we couldn't stay.

I remember we lived then in an old gray bus, but I might be wrong—that may have been a year and a half later, when we came back from Iowa and the landowners said my parents sold the trailer without ownership or permission. We lost the garage, the land, the investment. We got in our school bus, painted gray, and drove away again. I don't know which time we lived in what van or what bus. My memories blur and the addresses do, too, and so does the source of money. I just know we were always poor, though I didn't know it in those terms until later—my father used to say, "poor is a state of mind," meaning what? That he didn't consider us poor. I didn't know I wasn't "socially thriving" or that I was "destined for poverty," and I didn't care. I knew the landscape wasn't fully mine in either central Oregon or Iowa—I sought out wet places, ravines and ditches and creeks and rivers. I sought out shadows and shade. But I also played in red lava rock and scoria and pumice and sand. I learned landscapes full of beetles and crickets or sunfish and fat buzzing mosquitoes.

I do know how we got to Des Moines. We took the Greyhound, we three kids, ages nine, six, and three, plus my mom, to her mom's house. Grandma Marguerite mailed us the money to buy the tickets, and it took us three days to reach central Iowa, that old brick two-story. It was my first long trip on public transportation, and I wasn't afraid, just sleepy, and hungry, and pleased my mother had brought me an apple and purchased a packet of Marie's biscuits, a red sleeve of sweet cookies that made the whole journey a delight, plus those small dashes of color on the backs of seats, the press of the carpet-feel cloth on my face, sleeping in a pile with my siblings, going somewhere warm and safe, even as the darkness both inside and outside the Greyhound grew interminable, and frightening, and unknown. But the bus, and its recurrence in my life, is also another story.

In Iowa, we stayed with my grandmother for a few weeks before moving rent-free into my uncle's two-bedroom rental, and I was supposed to attend first grade, and then actually did. School had a structure I hadn't yet known, and sometimes I stared at other kids, whose habits I didn't understand. My mother took some classes at Drake University, and I attended Rice Elementary for a year and a half—the longest and most stable time I'd ever remembered (leaving my father back in Oregon), until later, when we lived in Grays River for five financially unstable yet nearly idyllic years, in the farmhouse where I came of age and where I lived the longest in my childhood—through middle school. I would later attend high school in three separate counties in two states, splitting one semester between Astoria and Naselle, and refusing to move at one point before that, staying, at the age of fifteen, with my strange, blue-nail-polished, big-haired neighbor and her hutch of floral and cat plates she ordered from a catalog, me living in her spare room with the shag carpet, painting my own fingernails blue to please her, so I could finish the academic quarter after my parents left to open a new gas station and tire shop by the delta of the large river—the Columbia—that separated one state from another. And here, I've skipped a bunch—moving back to central Oregon during second grade, then some indeterminate time in vans or buses, then Ocean Park, then Ilwaco, where we opened the Family Fun Center. I guess I haven't practiced enough, or the details bore me. Sorry, Laura. Let me try again.

Basic Needs: Shelter/Safety
Whenever my dad's latest entrepreneurial enterprise fell through and my parents embarked on some new business venture, the "investment" was prioritized first, and where we lived second. These in-between times—moving out of the duplex we couldn't afford or friend's rental we couldn't stay in because a real tenant was moving in—we'd live for a week, or month, or however long the business would require to bring in enough money for a deposit and first month's rent, in whatever livable space came attached to the business property. In Ilwaco, that was the van, plus the kitchenette

of the rental space, and my sister and I slept like princesses on the mattresses in the adjacent furniture store, where we very politely trespassed and borrowed the display furniture for the evening. Each night before bed, my mother slipped clean socks onto our feet, handed us our sleeping bags, checked to be sure no one was looking through the wide furniture store's windows, and opened the door between our rented portion of the strip mall and theirs, ushering us into bed nearest the door. *Don't wet the bed* was a given; I think my brother wasn't allowed because of his nighttime bloody noses. *Keep your socks on* was another given. My sister and I were giddy—we had a whole queen-sized bed to ourselves, a soft, dreamy mattress, nothing like a cot or couch or sleeping pad or bus seat!—and we happily woke when our mother came in before dawn, nudging me and lifting my sister, age six, out of the bed, pulling along the sleeping bag, and then running a vacuum over the floor so we left no trace of our footprints in the soft shaggy carpet. These were sweet days, and I don't know if my brother was cold sleeping in the van or on a cot in the Fun Center, but Raine and I were in heaven.

We later moved into an old rental house just across a wide field from the docks, so the smell of cotton candy and clam chowder in summer and fish fish fish all year, brought us through the tall grass to wander the sidewalk, coveting the tourists' fun vacation purchases, hoping we could entice them to come over to the other side of town where our family hosted billiards tables and Ping-Pong and Foosball and Pac Man, spend some money on chips and soda and burgers that arrived frozen and pink in a long plastic bag. We'd helped our mom paint a large wooden plywood sign, a mouse who had clearly taken a bite out of a nine ball—The Side Pocket, the matching shirts said—and we wanted our parents' place to be cool, to be the destination. After school, I invited other kids like me—the ones allowed to roam a bit—to come to The Side Pocket to hang out. We played a lot of Monopoly and Foosball, but at most my friends and crushes spent ten dollars total on snacks, and the overhead was so much higher than the income.

Once again, like the gas station and the one-stop mart and the tow truck business and the selling chamois or blankets at flea markets, it just didn't make it—and our Family Fun Center closed.

When my parents sold The Side Pocket, they set their eyes—and my somewhat-more-stable uncle Louie's $1,000 starter fund—on an old tavern building on a river bend in Wahkiakum County. And in the fall of that year, a few months into fifth grade, we moved from Ilwaco, where I'd lived throughout fourth grade, in the first real house we'd been in that I could remember, our fixer-upper rental near the fishing docks, to a combination of our van, once again, and the apartment upstairs from the tavern, accessible if you passed through a hanging blanket into our living room and kitchen—dingy, moldy rooms full of the smell of cigarettes and sweaty loggers—up the stairs to the bedrooms, two low-ceilinged uninsulated spaces that were damp somehow with river fog. I was grateful my parents found a rental house soon after, and we were only in the tavern apartment a month, at most.

It was late October, and we enrolled in school. I was in fifth grade, my sister in second. My brother, who'd had a fever when he was four and didn't attend school during the same short time I didn't—my kindergarten year, I'm not sure which for him—and though he was three years older, enrolled in sixth. School had already begun and friendships among classmates had formed. It was a small school, not more than twenty to thirty or so children total per grade, the district demographic families of settled Finnish descendants and a smattering of first-generation Mexican immigrants across two rural counties. My tall schoolgirl socks and braids and the moon on my forehead didn't help. We were automatically the weird kids, whose parents had bought the tavern, and our last name was Miller, so they called me Maya Budweiser.

It wasn't, in other words, the best of times. It was, in other words, the worst of times.

When the tavern closed due to the road sliding out and stopping the traffic, my father began the longest winter of drinking I remember, and the deepest of his depression. That was the year he threw a chair through the window, shattering the glass, and a toaster across a room. The year when I said to my sister, when I felt his mood darken, "Let's go upstairs and play!" and we'd shut the door and I'd turn up the music really loud so we could have a dance party. Later, as an adult, she confessed that she knew exactly what I was doing but pretended oblivion because "it seemed really important to you to protect me."

When finishing college, I taught for a year on the Lummi Reservation. I recognized my students had lives kind of like mine. When I drove them home from the after-school girls running club we started together—basically, me providing snacks then taking the girls on a two-mile training run down the road of the reservation, past the frybread truck, and back into the portable where

Ernestine's soup was ready for us to scoop into bowls (as long as we cleaned up after ourselves)—"Who are you staying with?" I'd ask them, knowing that was the question, not "Where do you live?" And they'd say, "My auntie so-and-so," who lives down this road, and I'd drive them there even though I wasn't supposed to drive students anywhere. It was too risky. It was too risky not to. If they walked the roads alone—long, dark, full of ferns—

*

Psychological Needs: Intimate Relationships, Feeling of Accomplishment

It seemed really important to me to protect them because I knew what it meant to go home to a place where the land was beautiful and only sort of belonged to you, and you to it, and you weren't sure what would happen, and that that relationship to the land, which was sacred, to be sure, would not protect you from other dangers. Protecting them sometimes felt like protecting myself.

*

Sorry, Laura. I'm supposed to be telling this in order.

By the time I was in fifth grade, I knew I wanted to be an educator and a writer. I knew what the hierarchy was, not because I had heard the concept, but because I perceived the lack of the top of the pyramid—not as a shape but as an absence, how you know when you see the sliver of moon, it suggests the rest of it that isn't there. When someone said a brand name and I didn't know the brand, or someone said Why are you eating that dark brown bread? and it was actually the best rye that week, from the food bank, not just white bread, or someone said *college* and I thought of it as that thing (a community college, large gray cement buildings) across the long, Megler Bridge, 4.1 miles toward Astoria, college something someone could attend if they had money to pay. But first, you'd have to reach the bridge. And then cross its main span, 1,232 feet of concrete and metal, the longest continuous truss in the nation. And then, at the other side, you had to have the money to pay the toll. And then tuition.

It all seemed somewhat impossible—college. I was happy if, each week, my mother would drive us to the library van, ten miles away. I was happy to ride a bicycle to the river in the afternoon and see the fish dart in the shadowed underhangs of alder, to take a book away from the noises of men. I was glad to pen notes in my journal, its pages cast in the fossil-like shapes of my hair's shadows.

*

We lived in the Grays River Valley for almost five years. After the tavern closed—which was right away, fall of fifth grade—my father pulled us from school all winter so we could make cash, make rent. That old story. We drove around the state, living in the van while our parents re-covered billiards tables, sold chamois in flea markets. When I was in sixth grade, my mother began to substitute teach. When I was in eighth grade, and my brother in ninth, he dropped out of school to work with my dad. When I entered ninth grade, my mother began teaching elementary for a private Catholic school in Astoria. It was 1993. Her salary was $15,000 a year, and a year later, we moved to be closer to both her job and my father and brother's new business, in Warrenton: towing and tires, operated out of a small rental building by the pilings of Youngs Bay.

Because my father doesn't like the "city" (which in his definition seems to be any municipality with a stoplight), we moved to Brownsmead, a small community twenty miles east, to an old, drafty rental house with peeling wallpaper. Right away the house felt haunted. I'm not sure if it felt haunted because it *was* haunted, or felt haunted because from the start I spent most of the time we lived there alone: my father and brother left early each morning for work, and my mother and sister went with them, to Astoria, where my sister could attend sixth grade for free at the private school where my mother taught. I took the bus to Knappa, where I completed one semester of tenth grade. At the time, I didn't know I'd be there only one semester. I thought I was making a new life. It was how we'd done it before, when we moved every few months during childhood: pack your box and get in the car, we're leaving. This time I had been allowed my bicycle, too, and we even transported furniture; I had also saved babysitting money from that summer to buy myself some clothes. My mother wanted me to feel like I fit in, so she took me shopping. I had mistakenly guessed, based on the earthy folks we'd met briefly in Brownsmead, a town on a slough, with a grange where women wore aprons and braids and skirts with boots, that this place was sort of "hippie chic." I splurged: one pair of leggings and a flowy rainbow top, plus one other floral shirt, at the Maurice's in Astoria. I was fifteen and felt extravagant and savvy, like I was headed for popularity, or at least blending in, but the earnest, self-contained kind.

I was wrong. When I arrived in my English class, the most popular, trend-setting girl wore tight jeans and a top that showed her cleavage, and told me drily, in a tone without a question mark, that our teacher was "kind of hot, isn't he." I didn't understand how an English teacher would be considered sexual, and I didn't really think he was, or could be—beyond the exquisite possibilities for new book recommendations. To me, he was our teacher. And there was another Maya in the class; she spelled it differently, *Mia*, and it turned out the teacher had said it incorrectly: it was pronounced Mee-ah, and she did not like this new girl whose similarly unconventional name came too close to hers. I decided to make a new space for friendship, outside of my classes, and begged my mother to let me join the volleyball team.

I had played volleyball in eighth and ninth grades and was decent at it in our last small town. I thought perhaps I would earn a spot on the JV squad and make friends with a few other less-popular, hopefully brainy, girls. But I accidentally somehow made it onto varsity, and that caused all manner of problems: boys noticed me; the teachers noticed me; it upset the hierarchy. That's also another story—the one that precedes a first kiss.

*

I used to teach students how to write thesis statements. At first, I somewhat fought it. I taught them to begin by writing a series of sentences they liked the sound of, or images they thought held overlapping patterns, or ideas that made them feel a buzz or hum. These could be their own or those of the works they were reading—they had to cite their sources, but they could worry later about how they fit together. Next, after this recording of buzz or hum, they would read their own sets of words and other students', to notice what questions the sentences might be collectively asking; then they'd see if they could organize their ideas, words, images into sets of answers or claims. I told students their theses could be explicit/directly stated, or implicit/implied, and that sometimes, even writing that made claims still never had a thesis. Sometimes it had a dominant impression. The problem with academic writing, I told them, was that it assumed a specific approach to understanding, or to curiosity—that there would be answers, and clear opinions, and claims. But *we* know, I said, and the "we" was important, because I included myself in the experience—*we* know that life isn't that simple. It's never that simple.

*

In Brownsmead, the first semester of my sophomore year, I kissed a boy, made enemies, and from my English teacher, who also taught me who the Counting Crows were and told me their lyrics were a form of poetry, I learned I could write something like that, too, him playing *August and Everything After* for us on repeat while we wrote our feelings in blue-lined notebooks. I thought every song was about me, or about me in some version of my life: *round here, something radiates*. I also learned, from my geometry teacher, of something called an *SAT*, a test you had to take before you could apply to college. I knew the test cost money I didn't have, but already I was thinking about elaborate stone buildings in England and Baltimore (where it was also raining, according to Adam Duritz), both equally unattainable in their distance from me, in Clatsop County, Oregon, where I was daily riding my bike to the slough after volleyball practice, even in the gathering dark, lying on the gray boards looking into the black water and dreaming up my unattainable Oxford future, when my parents said we'd be moving again, to Astoria, that it didn't make sense to live this far away from where everyone was spending their daily lives. And I refused. I said I had to finish the semester, at least, or I wouldn't get good grades (or credit!), and then I wouldn't be able to go to college. Bullshit, my father said. But then I was hysterical, screaming and crying on the floor, and they let me convince them I'd live with the neighbor lady to finish out the semester, then move in with everyone else in my family, in the duplex they'd rented in town.

So I lived mostly on my own for a few weeks (was it a month?), with the neighbor who barely noticed when I came and went, and I spent evenings painting my fingernails blue and doing geometry until the numbers blurred with the thick shag floor of her spare room and I fell asleep, my moon scar pressed into the carpet, the carpet pressing back like a future or a past, imprinting.

*

Self-Fulfillment Needs: Creative Activities and Achieving Potential

At Astoria High School, population approximately five hundred, they enrolled me in something called Honors English, based on my A grades on my transcripts so far. Honors English sounded like something out of a movie, and the best way to prepare for college, so I was excited to experience it. Would we write poetry, as we had with my "hot" teacher in Knappa? Maybe there were other poets alive today, besides the lyricists for Counting Crows. I hoped to learn about them. I was also allowed to take courses called electives. Before now, I'd been educated in small town curricula: sometimes these schools offered art classes, and other students, whose parents had money to purchase or rent instruments, could take band. My family's money was strictly for essentials, so a violin or flute or even a clarinet (cost listed here in descending order), remained utterly out of the question. Up to now, I'd taken occasional wood shop or drawing or painting, if it didn't cost an extra fee, and nothing else. In

Astoria, I looked longingly at the course catalog's various electives, including music classes, for which I was grossly underprepared, knowing that even in order to take choir, I would have to be able to read music. Many students had begun to acquire these skills in fourth or fifth grade. So I considered the others such as ceramics (but there was an $80 fee) and then saw Calligraphy: The Art of Lettering. I was ecstatic. The catalog informed me I had to purchase my own supplies. I had saved some money from haying and other rural chores and knew I could make some money babysitting kids from my mom's school, so I could afford the pens. And I could walk to Newberry's, a few miles from our duplex, to get them.

Calligraphy proved to be simple and delightful, and not as difficult as expected, and it was also creatively fulfilling—I found the fifty minutes sped by in what felt like ten, looping words around sketches I made in my large, unlined notebook, like bug trails on bark—but Honors English proved to be a different story. I could read books quickly and with excitement, writing lines down in my journal, but when I received my first formal essay back from the teacher, he had scrawled a red *C-* across the top.

I didn't understand what I had done wrong in my essay, and when I finally helped my teacher understand exactly how I didn't understand, he explained to me the concept of a thesis statement. Apparently, I had been writing journal entries and calling them essays all my life.

*

The following fall I was prepared to get prepared for college. It was my junior year, the one when grades really counted, when I would, presumably, take the SAT. But that fall, shortly after I began the semester, my parents informed me we'd be moving again. Soon. When? Whenever it worked out to finish up some things here. But when, on an academic timeline, I wanted to know. Semester? No—they couldn't be that specific. They weren't sure. It depends on when the house is ready for us to live in it, they said, and when we can move our things. (We took our things along with us now when we moved. There was more to figure out.)

This time, we were returning to the district where I'd attended fifth to ninth grades, the longest time span, but most difficult years socially, of my school experience. They said, "It'll be wonderful to go back to where things are familiar!" My parents hated living in town, in a duplex, and they'd found an acre of land they could buy—sure, it was on the highway, and sure, it had a house with only one bedroom, but we could make it work until they could build something larger. And my brother, who was eighteen, would live in an outbuilding—the large shed, and, they said, we'd be back in the country and not "that terrible, dark house in Brownsmead that none of us liked."

Again, I reasoned, and when it failed, threw a fit—I would not relocate outside of a timeline that worked for my GPA. Finally we resolved that my father and I would go over at the quarter—in November—and the rest of the family would follow. So I came "back" to my old class at Naselle High School, where I had the circumstance of having gone through almost a year and a half away from them, so I was a bit of an Other again, and this time, the distancing worked to my advantage. I knew I wanted to go to college, and I knew I was not going to get stuck in this place with a beautiful landscape but where the only future careers or lives most of us could imagine—fine lives, to be sure, but not all the options we should have—were stay-at-home mom, logger or fisherman, clerk at Okie's Market, or working the counter at Johnson's One Stop. Johnson's One Stop, where you could get the closest thing in the county to fast food, where my brother liked to buy corn dogs and greasy burritos whose meat was unidentifiable and which could have been anything, even a rat, fried in oil.

When the red-winged blackbird lit across the slough, settling on the cattails, its song trilling, I decided that I was going to college, no matter what, and these next two years I would do anything to make that happen. I swore to the moon on my own forehead, where I'd been baptized once in a creek confluence of salt to fresh, and I took my books to the shed and the forest and on the bus, wherever it was going. I joined cross-country and track to see more of the state, to increase opportunities. I watched the moon moving through its phases, and I said when I touched my scar that I would do anything I had to do to follow it out of here, to somewhere else where I could write it better, the parts we could see and those that were only suggested in the logged, scarred hills, covered in winter with clouds, in spring with foxglove, those flowers that clothe a clear-cut with their bright purple bells.

EVERYTHING I KNOW ABOUT "ORDINARY AND TYPICAL HUMAN BEINGS WHO MADE IT INTO HEAVEN" I LEARNED FROM THE MOVIE, *SAINT RALPH*

Ralph is fourteen when his mother, ill with cancer, slips—like a ray of sunlight through stained glass—into a coma. His father is already dead, killed in war, so Ralph lives alone, selling off wagons full of things to pay for groceries. But he believes in miracles: that winning the Boston Marathon would wake her, that he could really convince his crush to date him despite the million mishaps of puberty: his ejaculation in the public pool, burning down his house, smoking on Catholic school grounds, his near expulsion.

Each scene is framed by intertitles of feasts of saints: patron saint of fire, patron saint of forgetting, patron saint of whatever sin he's near committing until eventually Ralph takes a train to Boston.

No spoilers, people, you're going to have to watch it for yourselves.

I never went to Catholic school, but once I asked my mother to buy pajamas in a thrift store. They matched, green polka dots on white cotton, four dollars we didn't have for spending, and I didn't need them, I had a shirt or something I could wear to bed. Later we found a brown paper bag sitting in front of our house, note attached: *I wanted her to have them*; my mother furious with embarrassment and me feeling something like shame.

How proud Ralph is of his running, around the park at night, through the fields and past the factories with their smoking towers and the bay and the men in stocking caps, rubbing their gloved hands together. Ralph runs alone. He's already orphaned as any distance runner who knows she'll always be there with her legs and her breath, the town below her or around the next bend in the woods or in the stands or going about their little sins or miracles. Any distance runner comes to believe in the miracle of her own running, how it takes her out of town, away from death, and how it is quiet and how it is the best way to be with the body and how it lets her release the breath she's been holding in for years.

In one of my favorite Brigit Pegeen Kelly poems, the speaker says we're fools to believe the angels in a window are in ecstasy. She says, "they do not love the light." And when she says they do not love that light, she says, "As I / do not love it," and I become her,

> so sweet,
>> so good, the women say who bring [her] family money, but
>> I am not sweet or good.
> I would take one of the possums we kill
> in the dump by the woods where the rats slide
> like dark boats in the dark stream and leave it
> on the heavy woman's porch just to think
> of her on her knees scrubbing and scrubbing
> at a stain that will never come out.

When Ralph burns his house down, he's been wearing his father's army coat, holding a photo of his parents, drinking Scotch straight from the bottle. He falls asleep in his empty living room, all the furniture gone to the pawn shop, his fire spitting cinders.

The internet tells me the film was not met with critical acclaim, that it was full of clichés.

It does not tell me much about those bastards who reviewed it, but I can imagine they love abandoned houses, but only in theory, the way that people love poverty who have never been in poverty.

Sometimes you run straight into the mouth of abandon, letting things fall from you as you go. Sometimes you kill a possum and you take the carcass into the woods. Sometimes you poke a dead cow with a stick. Sometimes you believe in something fervently and sometimes you also know it will not end how you hope.

Sometimes you move from one town to another and you take only one box so your old house is empty and you have nothing material to show for the life you just lived.

I became a runner on the streets of Astoria, Oregon. I was fifteen and sick of moving. My mother was finally teaching, at St. Mary's Star of the Sea School, and suddenly had something called a *salary*. I was on my third high school.

The Astor Tower ascended into the gray sky beyond a small cemetery and up a tall hill; from there you could see everything. From there I almost kissed a boy I really liked, but I was shy. From there you could see everything.

You could see where Lewis and Clark holed up for a month while it rained, across the wide mouth of the Columbia; you could see the hilly city below you, the docks and the gulls and the seals and the ordinary and typical human beings and sometimes the whales with their prehistoric backs.

I could see straight into my future.

BALSAMROOT'S ARROW-SHAPED LEAVES POINT IN SO MANY DIRECTIONS AT ONCE

Just after my son was born, the medical staff read his one-minute Apgar score as 1. This reflected his too-slow pulse and his blue body. He wasn't moving, breathing, or showing any signs of life, beyond the faint heartbeat they could barely detect by machine.

Childbirth.org tells us, "A score of 7–10 is considered normal, while 4–7 might require some resuscitative measures, and a baby with Apgars of 3 and below requires immediate resuscitation." The Apgar test is generally done at one and five minutes post-birth and repeated only if need is determined. In my son's case, they repeated the test at one, five, seven, and ten minutes. After he was resuscitated, my son's scores improved, but not quickly enough. So he was X-rayed, CAT-scanned, his blood was drawn, he was given oxygen, lipids, and a cord was inserted in his umbilical cord in case he might need blood. The medical staff considered and decided against brain cooling, a risky but possibly healing measure taken when it seems the brain is in extreme danger. They kept testing to see if his organs would recover from the lack of oxygen. It took a few days before it seemed that they would.

It was two days before I held my son, and then he stayed in my arms only intermittently; I held him like he was a fragile egg. When finally we took him home, stable and "recovered," ten days from birth, I did not want to ever let him go again. But I felt from the beginning he had already seen darkness. I would feed him and love him fiercely, almost defensively, but always with a small tinge of fear that I would lose him. That unless he was with me, even when he is with me, he isn't quite safe.

Now my son is fine (mostly—he still experiences a lot of illness, an above average number of viruses each year, and his body, with its fragile immune system, is especially sensitive to emotional stress). For the first six months, he was evaluated regularly for residual neurological issues, and for the first four of those, his scores were always "behind target." We massaged him and sang to him and held him and I nursed him like it was a mission, and eventually, he was on target, and pretty soon, even his night tremors went away—you'd never know he had ever spent time in that fragile, mysterious place, and even my body sometimes almost forgets its fear, the way it clung like an animal to his light.

Psychologically, I knew my strange feeling of being somehow connected to him, of having his very being tied to mine, was due to maternal stress. I knew/know he's a separate person, that he can move through this world without my constant pangs of worry and pain.

But. In that first year, I read an article in *Scientific American* about microchimeric cells. *Micro*, from the Greek *mikros*, meaning small and *chimeric*, relating to a genetic chimera. *Chimera*, according to Merriam-Webster online, is "a fire-breathing she-monster in Greek mythology . . . [or] an imaginary monster compounded of incongruous parts . . . [or] an illusion or fabrication of the mind . . . [or] an individual, organ, or part consisting of tissues of diverse genetic constitution." This last definition occurs in the form of microchimeric cells, which often take up residence in the mother during pregnancy. Some of our children's cells migrate across the placenta into our bloodstreams, and sometimes lodge in our brains and organs. So, when we say we feel like our children are always a part of us, they are. And we, their chimeras, breathe fire in the face of any threat to our babies. We are (imaginary) monsters compounded of incongruous parts. We are illusions of our own minds. Any mother will tell you: learning to cope with all the possible challenges of motherhood can make a person feel, at times, illusive.

Maternal cells have also been found in children, as have cells from twins in their uterus-sharing siblings. But the most common occurrence is that of fetal cells in mothers. Robert Martone, the author of the article mentioned, suggests that harboring someone else's cells is strange. But Martone is a man and seems to see his own body as independent. When I, a biological mother of two children, read about this science, it seemed, well . . . obvious. It is another scientific confirmation (like the science that explains how mothers experience actual, sometimes acute pain when their babies cry) of something many mothers already know and feel: We hold our children inside us forever, for bad or good. Even after they exit our bodies and have to make a go of it on their own, or are pulled away from us by life circumstances.

Sometimes, when the sun is setting and I am walking on one of those basalt-based ridges above the Spokane River or Latah Creek, and the golden rays shine onto the arrowleaf balsamroot, I think of how that flower returns reliably each year, bright and beautiful, from its own roots, and also of how people native to this area used the plant as a funereal preservative, and I imagine my son's young body wrapped in those sage-colored leaves, returned to the dusty soil of the Inland Northwest. We named him Canyon. Laura says it is fitting because you can go down into a canyon, and then you can come back out. She was speaking of our grief and worry in those first days of not-knowing, how when I lay in a hospital bed she skipped her days at a lake cabin to come sit on those vinyl window-couches and read to me, to make me laugh and watch me weep. They left the plastic-sided bassinet in my room, and I saw it from the corner of my eyes and bawled because my baby would never lie in it. At night, I could hear the babies in the rooms around me crying for their mothers, who I imagined rising from their little spurts of sleep to lift their babies from those plastic bassinets and hold them on their chests.

I could not hear mine, but I imagined I could. He was upstairs, with the nurses I grew to know by name—how many children they had, how old, how many babies they'd held, which ones pressed for giving him formula and which would let me hold Canyon past his cruelly scheduled feeding time, me working again to make him nurse and him moving his lips into the shape of a latch sometimes and sometimes not trying at all until finally I gave up for the night and let them put my milk through a tube in his nose. Even after I was sent home, I returned every three hours to try again, driving back and forth across town and riding that too-shiny elevator with the brass bars and smooth marbled floor, pressing the number three so I could go up and tell Sandy, the woman at the front desk, "It's Canyon's mother," so she could call his nurse to ask if I could come back, and I'd go in, gown up, wash my hands, walk past all the other rooms full of babies to where my son was down the long hallway, sleeping in his own private lake of shadows, lights and cords all around him.

Researchers are still trying to decide the exact impact of microchimeric cells. Some evidence suggests that these cells, like tiny teams of healers, migrate to diseased areas of their host body and try to cure her. Other studies indicate the cells may, like other incongruent parent/host relationships, create problems, such as autoimmune disorders. And, the cells' link to Alzheimer's is another curiosity, as these cells occur more frequently in Alzheimer's patients. Could the fetal cells be trying to heal the mother's memory? Or maybe they are trying to make her forget, etching out a peaceful blankness where once she was fraught with worry. Worry over her son's state at birth, how he almost didn't make it into this world. What if he had stayed in the dim beyond, and I had spent the rest of my life carrying around those microchimeric cells, little Y chromosomes hanging out in my brain, my liver, my son's blood legacy traveling the byways of my body, but no other living proof that he had ever breathed?

For the first four days, before I went home, I learned about the hospital. I asked a lot of questions, like "What if a fire happens?" My night nurse Bree explained how they have big plastic coats, like rain slickers, with oversized pockets they're supposed to fill with all the babies from the nursery, tuck them each into their own slot and the nurses can move quickly down the stairs, get all the babies out. In the NICU they can take their beds, with wheels, right out the door, but if there is a real fire, the elevators don't work and they use the coats there too. I laid on my stiff mattress and imagined someone carrying our babies into the night, some crying, some sleeping, some wide-eyed and watching the flames curl up the curtains in the rooms where their mothers' things are burning: the cards her friends and relatives write, the book she's trying and failing to read, her spotless nursing camisole with its blue lace still folded in the bottom of the diaper bag. I imagined the mothers all out in the night in those open-backed gowns and skid socks, weaving through each other looking for the right infant. I imagined being strong enough to put on one of those long coats, fill my own pockets with babies, how I would want to feed them all to keep their little bodies still.

Before I had my own, I was never a baby person. When my daughter was born, I was grateful for her, and I loved her. She clung to me as if she were a joey, waiting to feel ready. She was mellow but not extrovertedly social—she wanted me most of all, to be close to my skin. And I became a "my baby" person. My daughter was almost three when her little brother was born, but she was not allowed to meet him right away. No children in the NICU. After nine months and two weeks of pregnancy, we had to explain to our eager daughter that her brother was born sick—he would not come home as we had promised. He would stay in the hospital, and I would bring him my milk, bottles and bottles of milk I'd load in a travel cooler and carry to the little fridge just outside his room, tuck them among the other bottles labeled for him. I would organize and reorganize the milk by date and time, hoping they were using it, knowing they were but feeling like it should be saving him faster. When we finally brought him home, two weeks later, my body had made so much milk I had to take home large bags of it—about two gallons from the ten days of pumping. It was as if my body knew all it could do was make milk. I made milk in ridiculous amounts. I made milk like the hills make flowers, in wasteful quantities.

At home I drank water, slept fitfully, cried, and pumped milk. Once, after about a week, still not knowing when he would come home, I lay on the porch and listened to the birth mix I'd created on my iPod. I had not had any time to hear it in the hospital—labor was too quick; I was in transition when I arrived and dilated to ten when rushed to surgery. So now I lay on my back in my red tube-top dress (I'd bought it to make nursing easy) and listened to Martha Wainwright in her tower of song and watched the blue sky come down through the maple leaves and their twinned helicopters and thought of how those winged pods could fly and hold seeds at the same time, spinning and spinning and letting the wind choose where they would make a new tree and how lovely that was and how Martha sang Leonard Cohen and how the two ached in the places where they used to play. I realized I had not yet cried that day—it was three in the afternoon and my eyes had stayed dry, and I cried for not crying. I went and tried again to nurse my baby.

There were other parents coming and going too. The fathers attempted politeness, muttered hello, but we mothers mostly looked down or away, not knowing how to meet each other's feelings of guilt or grief or ineffable worry.

I do not know what happened with those other mothers, or the mothers of children anywhere who, unlike my own, did not make it out of the hospital, or even out of the uterus, alive. The mothers will have to carry their ache, some lighting candles for their lost offspring, all the while perhaps harboring the microchimeric cells that will always wander their bodies, harming or helping the host. These mothers are mostly unaware of those living remnants of children they never raised. And I cannot know the end of their stories, of their joy or mourning or peace. I know our story has a happy ending—or a pleasant moment of peripety. And I hope against time, and unknowable future crises, that it stays.

My son is a child prone to injury—broken bones, split chins, gouged fingers. He's had at least three ER trips. He's always flirting with the other side. But he heals: he always forms himself whole again. Beautiful, like a perennial in its new season. Something that comes back.

Someday Canyon will walk in these hills with me and I will teach him arrowleaf balsamroot, the way his sister loves to recognize Oregon grape and wolf lichen and ponderosa pine. And maybe he will ask "What is it for?" and I will tell him all parts of it are edible. The seeds can be dried, or roasted, and ground into meal; the roots, stalks, and stems are best when young. It is for eating, and it is for looking at in the evening sun, and it is for sitting down next to on a lovely spring day like the ones when I walked while holding him inside my body, not yet knowing he would not be wholly safe, not knowing how the sky would look different and the arrow-shaped leaves would point in so many directions at once. When Canyon asks about the plant, I will tell him that like most plants that bloom, beautiful and brief, it is for feeding these fragile bodies we are given during our time on this earth. And then we will get down on our knees to dig up the roots, take them home, cook them slowly, and eat them, even if they are bitter.

HE WORKED AS AN ELECTRICIAN.
HE ENJOYED TELEVISION.
(HIS OBITUARY WAS PLAIN.)

After my husband's grandfather Ed dies, I buy our three-year-old daughter Frida Kahlo's Frocks & Smocks, a magnetic paper doll with clothing and accessories: monkeys and parrots, a paintbrush along with skeleton shirt and pants, onerous scarves and bracelets. Our daughter drapes these accessories in the wrong places: a bracelet on Frida's head, her monkey gripping the paintbrush and standing by Frida's easel, which also sports the disembodied head of Diego Rivera. Children, of course, are intuitive: this disarray is as Frida would have it if she herself could rise and drag her own floppy body across the coffee table, saying what Zoey does: "I like art and you like art, let's dance."

Then Zoey assumes a deep voice, sticks the stereo to the canvas, sings "I AM Frida Kahlo!" in the kitchen to the cats while I fold her baby brother's pants, roll his tiny socks together.

At the funeral, our son was seven weeks old, and we stood near his father's grandmother's grave in Osburn. When the baby fussed I would walk away from the small crowd into the headstones and watch the green mountains of northern Idaho shrug into the sky above us. This is where Ed worked as an electrician for Hecla Mining, the company that hauls silver up out of the earth, plugs the creek with lead and mercury. Hecla Mining, where my husband's father also worked, filling his lungs with airborne particles, to put his wife through nursing school.

This is part of our children's legacy. On the Hecla Mining company website, I find a rotating banner of photographs: one with a tractor scooping rock and mineral matter into a truck, one with a long tube used to ferry minerals up to the tower, one with four men and one woman standing in a row, all looking at the camera, all wearing hard hats and headlamps, mining coats against a backdrop of what looks like fractured rock spilling from a crack in a retaining wall.

I have tried to imagine this life, the life of my husband's family in Wallace, Idaho, in the heart of the Silver Valley where his ancestors migrated from North Dakota. I have tried to imagine his grandfather, who did not think about the term *social responsibility* but who was of the generation in which everyone had such a sense of personal responsibility that Ed himself hoarded his money and his belongings for years, knowing their use and their potential for disappearing, never to be reclaimed through any amount of hard work.

That summer, I have been teaching our daughter about death. She and I have been walking in that Spokane cemetery high above the river where we read aloud whose grave is whose, talk about what our spirits might do when our bodies stop breathing, until she loses interest, runs across the grass to find another pinwheel, those bright circles of light and wind. She counts how many, keeps track of colors. "The last one was purple and pink," she says. "I bet Papa Ed will like living with another man." She means he was lonely watching his television all alone in the retirement home, and she means Jesus or maybe a stranger whose head is floating in her mind, along with Diego Rivera's embroidered hat and the plate of watermelon and the large red heart you can imagine pumping blood, then suddenly not pumping blood.

When we used to visit Grandpa Ed at Northpointe Senior Living, I walked the hallways with Zoey, who was afraid of Ed and his small apartment, his wheelchair and his loud voice and blaring television. Zoey and I went looking for Cindy the dog who usually wandered upstairs. We'd find her lying by a fake plant or in another patient's room, like the room of the woman who kept a bag of dog treats and a crocheted blanket on her couch. Cindy would be sitting obediently at the woman's feet. When we walked by, the woman called out, "Come on in!" and Zoey, not quite three, obliged, plopping down on the couch and engaging in conversation like we knew everyone in the home. She had no boundaries between family and acquaintance, no reason to think we shouldn't walk right in. The door was open.

Back in Ed's room, my husband and his grandfather talked about the weather, the news station, the conspiracies Ed intimated were afoot in the assisted living facility. He'd shout his stories, and my husband would laugh and ask a question that Ed wouldn't hear, and he'd keep telling my husband about the nurses and how they would come at night and poke his arms, take his blood. I always wondered why he didn't want to open his blinds: he kept them shut tight, so the main light came from the television. But Ed knew things, and I imagine how rich his life was in physical detail.

My mother-in-law washed all of her father's clothes and made nearly daily trips to visit him. He had not been a good father. This is one thing she and I shared: fathers who were never emotionally available, who in many ways took for granted the care they received from women. But my mother-in-law dutifully transported Ed to his dialysis appointments, went back again and again to a horologist who fixed Ed's watch and fixed it again. It was made of Black Hills gold, with a leaf design around the face. I wonder if he liked it because of the value, or because of the leaves, or if he only wanted it fixed so many times to give my mother-in-law a sense of purpose. I know she loved him; I also know that during this time of caring for him she chewed her cuticles until they bled.

During my last visit with Ed, I was in the last trimester of pregnancy with my son. I do not remember what remarks Ed made, or what I said in response.

I'd had a good pregnancy. Our daughter had been born via Cesarean section after a relaxed natural labor, eight hours of pushing, and a transverse head that kept her from descending fully through the pelvis. I had a team of midwives for my first pregnancy, and this time I had a doctor with a good rate for VBACs (vaginal births after Cesarean). Still, when I arrived at the hospital already in transition, and the nurses placed the monitor around my abdomen, my son's heartbeat was pretty flat, so they rushed me to surgery. It's a common story: when it comes to childbirth, things often don't go as planned.

Oxygen deprivation during labor turned my son's body blue, and he was limp when they pulled him out of me. They called it birth asphyxia, and he spent a week and a half in the neonatal intensive care unit, tended by nurses and wrung through pricks and scans and X-rays, given lipids through a tube and hooked to monitors, surrounded by beeping screens and other babies whose mothers' bodies had betrayed them. Who felt (unfairly, unrealistically) it was their fault. Maybe because of mothers-in-law who gave us mothers disapproving looks. Mothers who maybe, like me, imagined their child dying there in the plastic box the hospital called a bed, wrapped in standard-issue blankets, pink or blue.

Once when I went for Canyon's care time, the nurse had him dressed in a little monkey-adorned onesie. He looked so much like a baby does in the world outside these sterile walls. He looked so . . . *real*. I felt angry, betrayed even: who was she to decide what his first clothing would be? And where did she get this outfit? It wasn't among the few things I'd put in his bed: my milk on cloths by his head so he'd know my smell, photos of my face and his father's face taped to the sides of his crib and the nursing pillow I kept behind the computer to pull down into my lap while I sat in those uncomfortable chairs and tried to get him to latch and suck without aspirating so he wouldn't have to get his milk through a gavage tube.

But finally Canyon left the hospital to come home, and the doctors suggested we limit his contact with other people, especially those with compromised immune systems. That meant Grandpa Ed, and so we didn't go to visit him.

We didn't go much of anywhere—the grocery store, the doctor's office, all contaminated with living organisms that could land our son back in the hospital. But we did go to the cemetery in Spokane. We went back sometimes two days in a row, and we continued to go there, for months, even years. The cemetery seems safe. We like the cemetery for its tall trees and cool grass, the scant amount of people who visit. And I find comfort in cemeteries during heat waves, tragedies—they are green even during July and August, when much of our city turns brown and withers, and when people fill the streets with their cheap flip-flops and cigarettes and sad eyes.

That first summer, we visit the cemetery, and a park or two, and keep Canyon out of the sun, away from too many people and germs. People are loud, even the birds swooping seem to be diving at my head. I like the trees—they are still, quiet.

When Ed died we went to Idaho to that small plot on a hill where I wondered again what sorts of things Ed knew that he could tell me now. I wanted to ask about keeping his blinds closed in the nursing home. Maybe the pavement outside his window was too gray and flat after decades of the pine and larch-covered earth, slanted to sky. Maybe he was thinking of electricity, how it is a transfer of energy into a form we can use to make things tick and go. And maybe, in the end, before his spirit left Spokane it stopped to see Canyon in his bassinet next to my bed.

I keep thinking about mining—how we extract mineral from rock. A rock is made up of two or more minerals, as a baby is a combination of DNA. Mineral from rock becomes part of the daily workings of our lives—televisions, cell phones, hangers to put our clothes on when we're not wearing them, when they hang like a memory of the day we may have lived in them. A memory like energy, something that cannot be created or destroyed. Can a memory be created, or is it just a transfer of experience—based in the physical world—into our brains? Can a memory be destroyed? My thinking is confused: it mixes mythmaking and physics; it mixes my thoughts of death with my feelings of motherhood. My brain fails me. I want back the rawness of the not-knowing, of patterns of the sensory and mental worlds still a broken kaleidoscope, still a pile of magnetic clothes you can arrange however you like.

Back in the cemetery, it is evening, and the stones throw long dark columns across the grass. Zoey says, "The earth turns away; the sun goes down." She knows the science, but she is still figuring out the language. Or maybe she knows the language and not the science. Maybe she knows things like Ed knows them, or Canyon, being closer to the beginning or end, with less to muddle her relationship to light and shadow.

She runs through the gravestones like they are trees. She does not think of the bodies beneath us, of the soil and rocks and their other lives. She does not think of the other grandfather buried here. She might be thinking of her skin, the way the wind feels against it. She might be thinking of the butterscotch scent of these tall pines. She might be thinking of Frida Kahlo. I don't know. I think, when I die, I would like to be cremated, my complex cellular matter made into a simple substance. Maybe put in a river where the fish will swim in and out of my body, my body will swim in and out of them. The sky is turning now, and I am nursing the baby on the ridge where the wind picks up voices from down below. The wind lifts them like seeds or spiders, carries them to us where we sit waiting.

LETTERS TO FRANCESCA WOODMAN FROM SPOKANE AND FARTHER WEST

After my son's birth, my brain struggled to feel like my body belonged in the world. It wasn't postpartum depression so much as postpartum departure—the creeping feeling that no one living could understand. I began to write letters to the late photographer Francesca Woodman, who I imagined could hear what I was saying. She "got it" about the permeability between this world and the next; her images felt familiar to me, her mind. Speaking to Francesca, I pretended, would return me to speaking.

I. After a Night of Fog
Sixteen degrees. The trees are skeletons standing on their sides, whisking clouds, stark and not staring, their eyes covered in frost. Do the dead get cold, Francesca, in their black-and-white dreams? If I were you, I would be perfectly content sitting in a river, watching snow cover the rocks that stick out, cold enough the current can't melt these stone islands. Do you get to choose? Or is death itself the last choice? My daughter asks where her infant brother was before he was here, and how he knew to come into my body, of all bodies. She knows he was out there, as if a person is not his skin. I have felt like this, too, but I can't remember it perfectly. When I was a child my parents took few photographs. There is one in which I am walking past the view of the camera, behind my

brother, who holds a string of fish. I am eight and shirtless, and my hair reaches the belt of my jeans. I am glancing sideways, as if the person behind the camera has caught my attention, but only for a moment.

II. A Retrospect

Your photos are like the places I used to live: the walls not wholly walls, the floors with boards opening to other worlds. I am sure my parents never worried about things like lead, asbestos with its microscopic fibers making their way into my lungs, my pores. They say if asbestos is wet it can't affect you. Where we lived, everything was always wet. No wonder I feel so at home here: the bathtub in our old farmhouse filling with silt-water during the flood, its scratched bottom like a floodplain after the water goes back to its dark source. It's the departure that makes things clear, like the leavings in a tea mug, muddy and thereby alive. When it left, I always wished I could go too—wherever it came from being beautiful and strange and full of the power I felt in my own belly, the power of current and a whole field laid down in awe. Crop circles never got to me—what of a pattern in which only part of the crop lies flat? The river decimated the whole thing. It was miles of soggy grass, old fences, barbed wire you wouldn't see until it pierced your flesh. That kind of flattening. The kind that gets into the houses. There's nowhere you're completely safe.

III: Telling Her About Drowning

When I am four I nearly drown in the ocean.

It's easy. One minute you're playing like any child will play, hopping that fine line of foam that advances and recedes. Your ankles are white like the sand dollars you skipped across still water, down shore where your mother sits reading a book. You're having fun. In a minute you will turn at some sound (a gull or bark or dropped shell or heave of cloud), and the wave will take you. Your mouth will fill with grit, and jellyfish, the salty tails of kelp, until you are an alluvial throat closing. You will want to see and be blind to seeing. And then, the light will be whale-fin wonderful: lit flesh between small bones, like that in its small openings, the strip of sun like morning, your brother will grab and rescue you, your wrists bruised where he dragged hard to wrest you from the moon-pull, its stiff grip and lucid tune. You'll have wanted to sing. You'll almost have known the song.

When I wake I am standing over myself, and the jetty stretches out behind me.

IV. The Counties of Southwest Washington

These old towns have a lot of broke-down houses. Floors falling through and basements that want you to collapse into them. Will you walk up the stairs? Peer around that corner? There's porn here, and needles, a vagrant's been sleeping on an old tweed couch, arms ripe with mushrooms. You want to stay until night, see if he's friendly. We're all transients anyway, you tell yourself, but know the danger in strewn newspapers. A mouse scurries from the wall to the other wall. You light a match and look in the closet.

V. From the City in Which My Children Are Born

You would have liked it here, all these old buildings kneeling in the dirt, getting mica on their knees while they lose their mortar to ice and the way you could stand on their roofs and let your eyes fall on the snow that piles like bricks in the middles of streets, trains cutting up hills with their freight. You can hear them from miles away, their seismic shaking and a tremor in your bones. In autumn you feel weightless and drive to Couer d'Alene to swim, your body floating for hours with the blue gown above you open, saying your name while jet planes carve their initials like lovers. The summer my son was born, fire burned up Wenatchee and the wind came east and the air filled with the smoke of other people's trees while I drove back and forth to Deaconess, my son there in the NICU, waiting for me to arrive. The chair was black and hard-backed and the nurses always prepped the pillows for me with crisp new cases. I would worry about my section stitches opening, what was left of my insides spilling while I held my baby, tried to teach him to put his mouth to my leaking nipples, my dress dropped from my shoulders, my breasts shameless. Above his plastic cradle the monitors never stopped beeping, little Timmy in the next bed would cry for milk and mine would let down and my son would turn away and begin to scream or sleep until we gave in and let him have his through the tube in his nose. Outside, the smoke hung like someone else's unworn wedding dress and I'd stand on the curb and wait for my husband to bring the car around. On the news they said our air quality was moderate to poor so we kept the windows closed. I wanted to tell you more about those buildings, how some have spires like castles and how you could probably fall from one and keep falling right into spring.

VI. January 19, 1981

On this day I am just past one and a half and my mother has written all my one hundred words on the inside flap of *The Foot Book: Dr. Seuss's Wacky Book of Opposites*, and I am saying things like *meow* and *apple*, running around in the Oregon drizzle with the ocean scratching its foam words all over the sand, erasing and writing and erasing them again so no one will ever know quite what it meant to say. Somewhere on that other coast you have decided it is over.

VII. Summer, 1979

It was the *body* I walked through to reach you. It was the body that broke, the mind still whole, the ligaments suffering their brief stretch, a boy balancing on a tightrope. Here, come with me. There is a turn here, a dip through the trees to a valley where the elk have just left. Their hides kept time with the rain, left a glimmer of where they were. If I could have run, I would have run there. It was like moving through water. My veins whole but still. This was the map corner where memory is made: the long muscle on the back of my thigh, the fetal position, then child's pose, me on all fours, the rise to stand, head bent and looking down at the piles of scat they left. It's called droppings, like something holy come from the clouds. Things glimmering and brown. You can tell a lot from what they eat. But standing, my arms feel a vision coming on, their hairs rising like the grass, everything turned to seed, seeding, the air thick with future. A white flash. It's your dress, printed with flies, the kind you catch a fish with. The fireweed has gone rabid behind you. I feel like you were standing in the water. You've already begun to die the day I am born.

VIII. Interior Geometries

I, too, grew tired of them trying to make sense of it. Let it be a covered bridge, a river beneath writing its slow calligraphy. Let it be a girl, not swimming, watching the tree roots stretch free from the bank. Let it be light on the poplars. Let it be my mother's cash box filled with small bills and food coupons, *do not fold or spindle*, the string of fish my brother brought home in a bucket and cleaned on the cracked cement of our basketball court, moss springing up like a facsimile of roots between the chinked slabs. Let it be the clothes we leave home when we move out. Let it be a bird against the sky when the sky darkens before the clouds split. Let there be no Greek gods, or signs saying what is dangerous to eat. Let the long slatted ceiling of the covered bridge be like my ribs, or not like my ribs, or not like anything. Quit coming back here. There is nothing here for you.

"NAPOLEON IS SO SMALL AND HIS HORSE IS SO HUGE"

There was often a grow light in the closet or shed, or PVC pipe clipped with plastic arching over young starts, or rows of black containers filled with slender stems in the greenhouse, or marijuana woven in among the tomatoes, a round cookie tin full of dried cannabis buds on top of the fridge, my father rolling a joint in his corner chair every night, but the first time I intentionally get high I am in my late thirties, married seventeen years, and a mother to two small children.

My friend does not know this when he grins slyly and hands me, now a professor and author, a small gift, saying "I bought this for you." Where I come from you accept anything that's valuable and free, and you don't complain (even if you're embarrassed at charity), so I take the joint. I no longer need to worry so much about the ramifications: I stopped nursing my son over a year ago, I'm no longer a person without access to resources, and anyway, marijuana is legal now in Washington, and I figure I'll probably regift it, so there's no need to admit I'm a weed virgin.

I say, "Thank you," and slip the Obama Kush into my pocket, thinking how I'm away from my children for the first time since my son's birth, four years ago. (My husband has left us many times, for personal adventure, coaching clinics, coaching travel . . . he, it seems, is always gone. And I cannot believe the freedom of using all my limbs.)

Then I walk back to my Airbnb in the dark, under the full moon, arm linked with my friend Ellie's arm. The air smells of blackberries and ocean and tall fields gone to seed but not yet cut. It's one of those perfect summer nights you remember being a teenager and are ready to make the kind of mischief a teenager makes. I'm at a coastal writers' retreat, and I'm supposed to be writing. Instead I've been wracked with mom-guilt, watching a doe and her fawn groom one another in the mornings. I'm supposed to be working on a project that taps into what I know of my paternal grandmother, who died from cancer of the uterus. I'm trying to write prose, for the first time.

And I'm stuck.

I decide to smoke the pot.

*

My dad self-medicated every day. That's what my mother eventually took to calling it: cigarettes or pipe tobacco throughout the day, beer in the afternoon, a carefully rolled joint every night. By the time he fell asleep in his chair, TV blaring, he was fully and totally medicated.

My first two initials are MJ. Being born in the 1970s on the Oregon Coast, during the Carter administration, means I come from a setting likely for getting high. My parents had a video camera with real film, and the home movies, video they've transferred from the reels to VHS, show hours of the green leafy footage: the blackberry- and salal-covered hills of Manzanita, the lush garden of marijuana under grow lights in the apartment upstairs from their gas station. The number of minutes the camera lingers on the pot garden versus the number of minutes the camera lingers on my brother, or on me, makes the artistic focus quite clear. Shortly after I learn to sit up, the camera breaks.

*

We light the joint. "This smells like my dad," I say.

"I can't believe you've never smoked it!" Ellie says.

"Because my dad smoked it *every day*." He smoked in the corner, I tell my two friends, from a pipe or joint. He drank beer, one after another.

We each take a hit of the joint. I'm new to it, but I know exactly what to do. I'm good at it on the first try. I don't even cough. I grew up watching my dad, breathing his smolder.

"I can't feel anything," I say, as my friends notice effects. "Do you think it's not affecting me? I wonder if I need more, because of all the secondhand smoke in my formative years?"

My friends laugh. "I'm not sure that's how it works," they tell me.

Later, I look it up. Studies suggests that under concentrated conditions, secondhand smoke *can* have effects. I don't know this yet; I want to try more anyway. I take another hit.

"My freshman year of college," I explain to my friends, "I felt a little anxiety during fall quarter. Maybe I was addicted to pot and going through withdrawals." It's an interesting hypothesis. It could also be that I was not from a family of college-going people: my father, at fifteen, dropped out of high school to live on the streets; my mother, in her early twenties, left college to go west and hook up with my dad (she later went back to school—I was six); my brother quit high school during freshman year, later earning a GED; my sister completed several quarters of an AA degree but decided academia wasn't for her.

*

I remember being so young I thought my father was good.

Scratch that. I never thought he was all good. Back then, I feared goodness—church, the capital F father, the one my mother had known as a girl in Des Moines, Iowa, in the Bible Belt, back there where she came from, the seat of goodness, her Catholic family, before she hopped a van west, turned green as the jeweled coast, sold and burned my first home to the ground, followed my father to La Pine, Oregon, so now here we were in this sagebrush pine bark witches lichen scarred tree orange light landscape, the one full of dust and mica and red rock on the road that had cooled so slowly you could see where the air bubbles escaped.

It was dry, so we built our worlds in the sand. While my father was off trying to make a go of it again, all day we built forts in the woods behind the garden, out past our little rectangle of green, out back where we took our photographs with Burger King crowns as the King and Queen of Compost, the stench and heat of it rising and mingling with the clothesline, its musk and fiber smell, and the outhouse, the slim little building we only used in summer for number two, unless we could go to a friend's house and sneak and use the flush toilet, which we all preferred.

All day while our mother weeded or sorted beans or pinned sheets and underpants to the line or chopped wood, we rode imaginary unicorns into the twiggy woods. Sometimes Seth would come by and bring strawberries, and I gave him my favorite, highly valued Wildlife Treasury photo of a tarantula. We ran around the track together in PE, and once he stuck up for me when Mrs. Rosemary asked Why does she stare like that? He was my one true love.

When the sky began to darken and we'd eaten our fill of whatever was ripe in the garden, when our shorts were a little more torn and our feet one callous harder, we'd hear the gravel on the main road spin out a little, spraying away from a set of tires, and then music, sometimes, Dire Straits or CCR, *We do the walk of life*, and we'd drop our toy metal cars and sprint down the driveway, shouting "Daddy Daddy Daddy Daddy," running alongside his car when it came into sight, and he slowed so we could keep up, and he rolled down the windows and he grinned, and we called out Daddy Daddy and jumped up and down until his car stopped. He always lifted up my sister first—she was the smallest; and if my brother had stuck around, not down the street on his bicycle, my father would pat his back or punch his shoulder, or this is how I remember it, and sometimes he smiled at me and we'd follow him into the house, the smell of bay leaves and beans.

I thought he was a little bit good, then, or at least I'd been trained to sing it like a song, Daddy, Daddy, as if there was something he'd do for us, or with us, when he came in. He'd crack another beer and sit in his chair and have a smoke, and we'd scatter back to wherever we could be most quiet, the crunch of the car tires still ringing in our ears.

*

The Obama Kush is really nice, once it takes effect. I can feel my head grow heavy, my fingers weighing fifty pounds each. But it's a happy heavy, a whale heavy. I'd float if I were in the strait. My fat feels good, like a body you love.

Then everything is funny, hilarious. I can tell that it's not really funny; it's just perception. I try not to laugh, but tears are rolling down my face. You can imagine the dialogue. I'm looking around the room, scrutinizing each piece of décor: "Where do you think that pond is from?"

"And who did that needlepoint?"

"There are too many lamps in here. Why are there so many lamps?"

Then I'm hungry. "I need a snack. Someone get me a snack."

"There's chocolate," says Ellie.

"I don't want that," I say, whiny.

"Sesame sticks?" Laura offers.

"No," I say.

"Pizza?" says Laura.

"Yes, give me a piece of pizza, but just tear it off. I don't want a whole piece."

"Do you want it microwaved?" Laura says.

"I don't *like* microwaved pizza," I say. "You know what I don't like even more? Microwaved chicken. It's the worst. No one should put a bird in a microwave. Even in small pieces in an unrecognizable form."

"Okay," says Laura. "But I touched your pizza." She knows I don't like sharing germs. She's being considerate, but I snap at her.

"I don't care. Why would a person *care* about that?"

I say a lot of sarcastic meanish things, and I can hear them coming out of my own mouth, and I can't stop them. "OMG, I'm *mean* on pot!" I say. Then: "My dad was so mean all the time."

*

It's December 2006. I am at a bar in grad school, and Saddam Hussein has just been killed by hanging.

He has dark bushy eyebrows, a silver-flecked beard, a face like he's seen things, and dark lines, too, under his eyes, where his guilt rests like two shallow ponds of mosquito larvae.

Saddam Hussein has just been hanged, and I have not watched

a single video clip of it because Saddam Hussein looks remarkably like my father. And in the years following, I will struggle to write about my father, because when I do, I imagine my words could be killing him. It makes no sense, but that's how it is: once I could really imagine my father dying, I felt I needed to go ahead and wait to write any more.

Before the hanging, I wrote a lot about my father, even wrote him dead sometimes in my poems; like every good undergrad I'd read Plath and like every high school girl I'd made out with a boy my father didn't know about and probably detested: mine was named Kodi and he had dark eyes and he kissed me first, in the library; and like every small-town middle school girl, I'd laid on the bed of the neighbor, whose parents never paid attention, and we listened to the hair bands, Poison and Guns 'N' Roses and also Kurt Cobain and I knew what Daddy Issues were, and I knew how cliché it was to write them. Still, I had them, so I wrote them, I wrote my daddy dead, until Saddam Hussein was hanged and I could imagine the rope around my father's neck.

I think a dead parent gives us permission to write more about them, and my father isn't dead. Thinking of him dead makes me think of him most alive: laughing, playing pool, that serious face focused on a task with a clear and audible ending, the crack of a cue stick to a smudged white ball, knocking a forest green one into a side pocket.

My father wore Carhartt or Key pants then and now, suspenders to hold them up, and work boots. He wore navy blue polo shirts that always got a little dark in the armpits, and before his eyes went bad, he was one hell of a pool player. He had so many trophies from tournaments—the kind you see in trophy stores, all sizes, mostly large, with the shiny blue plastic inlays between the tinselly gold or silver columns, Greek-like, with titles of First Place and Second Place Team and First Place Cutthroat.

My father said pool was easy, it's all basic geometry, and even though he dropped out of school when he was fifteen he taught us the angles and how to hold a cue and how to roll it on the table to check it for curves and how to crack the ball so hard when you break that the bigs and littles roll all over the table. We all learned bank shots and how to draw the cue ball back so it stops short and you don't scratch, and when I was nine he gave me my own cue, one that you can untwist and put into the red plush-lined, leather case and bring with you when you go to the billiards hall.

*

I'm telling my friends about my first kiss. School library, my boyfriend Kodi. My father didn't know about Kodi, because he was Black. I have complicated feelings about my girl-self then too. She clashed with her father; she still wasn't brave enough to tell him about her boyfriend. I am disappointed in her. I am also tender toward her.

My friends and I are feeling very open, sharing all kinds of things about our pasts, about our deep insecurities. Maybe it's the Kush. Leafly.com notes the strain highlights as "appropriately channel[ing] the President's famous message of 'Change' as it invigorates and inspires." I'm feeling that, thinking how profound and ironic it is that my first joint was named after a president against whom my father has made multiple racist remarks. I'm thinking how my mother warned me to keep the story of my first kiss from my father. And I'm thinking of how, later, the first boy I let slip his hands up my shirt had the same first name as my father, and all of this is very very funny, like I'm a teenager.

I stop laughing to share: "He knew what to do with his lips," I tell Laura and Ellie. We all dissolve into childlike laughter, girl-laughter. It lasts for what feels like hours.

"Why is Napoleon so small and his horse is so *huge*?" Laura says. She's staring at a painting on the wall and we all erupt into giggles. "Sorry, Maya, I know you were saying something important. But seriously, you guys, that horse is just *so huge!*"

We look at the horse. It really is huge. And Napoleon is just a boy, hardly old enough to rule anybody. What a cultural history, we say. What a hard time for such a small boy. Europe has had some serious issues, we say. No wonder everyone came to New England. Everything was very messed up over there. Then we came and messed up everything here. We brought all that mess right across the ocean.

*

In our refrigerator, and in our pantry, there was my father's food and then there was our food. Our food was often beans, rice, vegetables from the garden, powdered milk, raisins, berries we'd picked, and those hard oat lumps my mother called cookies. My father's food was real milk, Grey Poupon mustard, burgers in a Styrofoam container brought home from the bar, and Braunschweiger.

My father ate a lot of things like Braunschweiger, that foul-smelling meat in a tube. He was from Germany, and this was something he brought with him.

Braunschweiger, named after the town in Germany, is a spreadable, raw pork sausage. In America, it is usually made from liver, and comes in a plastic casing clipped on the ends. My father ate it spread on white bread, from the store, with mustard and tomato. It has a grayish pink, *spreadable* look.

Brauns smelled like canned shit. I would never say that. I was aware of God like someone who looked in the windows or through your clothes, through your skin, through your best intentions. My mother had told me about God, how when she was a girl she loved the stained glass set in high wooden arches. I was four, and I thought if I could be very good for a very long time, that maybe I would be good enough to see a church like this. I knew swearing was wrong, and somehow I had it in my mind that swearing even in your own head was wrong, so sometimes when my brother's friends sprayed gravel at me from their bike tires or led me into the woods and tied me to a tree and left me there or when my father was eating Braunschweiger and I wanted to say *Shit*, I didn't, instead I tried to hold it on my tongue, to force it back down where it came from, that dark place in the pit of me I was trying and trying to banish. I'd sing a song to get the words I felt out of my consciousness, and I'd apologize to God, whoever he was, and I'd try to list the things I'd do for penance: drink the powdered milk, not my father's when everyone was asleep; eat the beans, though they needed salt; pull the weeds in the garden, not the marijuana; save a stink bug from my brother's homemade heat chambers (glass jars placed over them in the sun, so the bugs would go limp). I followed him like a spy and I took all the jars away, and I tried not to feel angry, I tried to feel something else, pure light and goodness, I tried to think of where my grandmother was, in heaven, or back in Germany in a grave, or wherever the best part of her lived now.

I also thought of my uterus; I knew the word from the stories of her diagnosis, and I hoped mine would not end up like hers, and that I would be alive later to know what happens after, what else a woman can be.

*

"I'm going to bed," I tell my friends. "My body weighs 7,500 pounds." I'm going to swim to bed like a whale and think about my grandmother's reproductive organs.

*

I never met my paternal grandmother, Carmen. She died when my father was a boy. She had cancer of the uterus, that organ we use only to grow children. If it were 2016, maybe they'd just remove her uterus. Maybe the cancer had spread too far. I don't know much about that.

I know that my father, as a boy, loved his mother Carmen. I know this because in his slim black briefcase of papers, he keeps all her documents—her passports and American papers, her birth certificates from before she married his father and they had him, the changed documents that suggest to us she may have married him to escape the war in Germany, that my sister and I hypothesize this makes clear that she was a Jew, that our grandfather, American military, was her ticket to her life and her young son's life, my uncle Fred, only half-brother to my father.

This is how I see him: when my father was five, before his mother fell ill, she used to hold him and stroke his hair and read to him on the floor of their apartment. His father was off doing military things, whatever his work was, or smoking those sweet fat German cigars with the men from his unit, or playing poker, which he taught my father later, in the evenings sometimes. But this is the daytime, and they've just read some picture book. My grandmother had her boys—Fred, Barry, and Louie—and she left them to each other for a while, while they shot marbles in a circle on the floor, and it rained outside, and she made them sandwiches of sausage and mustard and tomato, and sang to them in her sweet German voice, some lullaby, and even though they were too old for it, and they couldn't talk with their mouths full, and even though it was just afternoon, they hummed the words: *guten abend, gute nacht*, and their mother called them her little sausages, wursts, and hummed *ich liebe dich*, the only words I learned from my father, the ones he spoke sometimes into the air when he was drunk at night and we were small, the ones for the mother he missed, the ones we always thought were for us.

WHERE MY MOTHER NEVER SET FOOT

Do not walk in front of me, I might not follow.
Do not walk behind me, I might not lead.
Walk beside me and be my friend.

In my first years as a mother, I taught at a Jesuit university, where there was no maternity leave policy, and mothers were hailed only as religious icons, as vessels for Jesus, not as practicing artists/academics. When I ran into colleagues, they'd ask about my children but not my work. I wondered if they thought I brought my children into the classroom with me, or if they thought I was forsaking them to be here, working. My mother had been raised Catholic, and suddenly all of her daily guilt, and her duty, and later her problematic relationship to guilt and duty, made more sense. The ways she didn't genuflect so much as kneel into my father's bidding. The ways she saw the Father as superior to the Mother. The Mother as a holy ship, as caring for children, as receiving all wounds so the father could shine.

This could be my mother's university, I used to think, in my early days there. *It's not mine*, with its two-spired Catholic church, white crosses on the top of each spire lit at night like guiding stars. You can see it from anywhere on the college campus, from most places along the riverfront trail that meanders past the sprawling lawn of the university into downtown. I often used it as a reference point when giving directions to students: the church squats kitty-corner from my office like a Gothic-faced origami frog or like an architectural version of the pop star Madonna, lying on her back, with her spiked breasts pointing up. Or the towers are double-phallic emblems piercing the sky with their crosses, saying Here, crucify this, clouds, bring down on us your milky rain, your kiss of renewal, your global version of evolution in the form of snowy winters, then birds singing of spring too soon, too late, too brightly. (I didn't say all of this, but I wanted to. I said it only to the poets.)

When I turned my car from Sharp Street onto Astor in the morning, hoping to find a close parking spot, the church lay ahead of me. When I went into Robinson Hall to check my mailbox, retrieve my photocopied assignments to pass along to students, the church squatted to the south. When I walked to College Hall to teach my courses, the church waited to my right, its stone steps angled toward the carved wooden doors. It's beautiful architecturally, sure, but what I noticed most is how it tolls a bell on the hour, how the dinging reminds me of the fullness of my mother's voice calling me when I was ten. I could have been anywhere. I was probably in the garden where I'd been lying beneath the tomatillos, watching the sun set. I loved the sound of the word *tomatillos* in my mouth, the shapes of the green fruits encased in their translucent papery skins. I loved the salsa I knew we'd make with them later, its slightly tart taste. The spiders spun webs from the tops of the tomatillos down to the strawberries, gliding along them like thistle down carrying its seeds to the wind. I would lie still so the spiders didn't mind me, and those webs, too, were a fine screen for the sunset. I could lie in the garden for so long, curled like a cat between the roots of one plant and the next.

It was never my university, though I taught there seven years. They hired me the same month my mother was laid off from her teaching position at St. Mary Star of the Sea School, which we found out, a year into my own employment by Catholics, would close its doors that June. My mother called me to say it was in *The Daily Astorian*, nobody had bothered to tell her, could I believe it? The article said how the school had been operating in the red for too long; the current economy necessitated closure of a lot of businesses, and sadly, many private schools were following suit. It said it wasn't a sudden revelation. Indeed, two years prior they already had to cut one teacher, and my mother volunteered herself. She had learned of a tumor in her pituitary gland, learned her body was producing too much growth hormone. The condition is called acromegaly—also known as gigantism—and it causes a host of complications. For my mother, the symptoms had manifested in almost all ways possible: she had developed diabetes, had the typical joint pain, enlarged bones of the face, enlarged hands and feet, skin tags, enlarged jaw, and swollen tongue and lips. She'd had many of the symptoms for years, but they came on slowly, and acromegaly is uncommon, largely unknown by many in the medical and lay communities. By the time she was diagnosed, my mother needed surgery immediately. Then, she would need time to recover after surgery, so she wasn't sure she'd be able to teach in the fall.

I was eight months pregnant when she had the surgery, and eight months pregnant when I interviewed for the job at the Jesuit school I'd begin just weeks after my daughter was born. My mother's tumor, surgery, and subsequent time of healing obviously overshadowed my pregnancy and my daughter's birth. While I felt horrible for my mother—brain surgery is certainly not a desirable way to begin your summer, end your fifties, or continue your life—I also felt cheated. I'd hoped my mother would be around after my daughter was born, but making the eight-hour drive to where we lived, near my husband's family, now seemed impossible to her. For months after the surgery, she had trouble concentrating for more than a few minutes at a time. Our phone conversations were stilted; her short-term memory was, at first, quite fuzzy. She often repeated herself, forgot what I'd told her the day before. It was a normal part of the healing process, but it was also frightening.

My teaching at a Catholic university during these first months of healing seemed, somehow, kismet. I thought about my mother's upbringing in the Catholic faith in Des Moines, Iowa, her seven brothers and sisters, her all-girls high school, all the rituals and rites she'd been a part of before she left college, moved west, and met my unconventional father with his long hair and tow truck, the gas station they'd lived in on the Oregon Coast. Like all mothers do, my mother had lived a whole life before children. If she could have had a conversation, she could offer insight into these strangely shiny students I was teaching, these young men and women whose lives had led them to a college on a river, to a professor carrying her past like a kerchief in her pocket.

My mother always said the archdiocese—the governing church body in Portland—"had it out" for Star of the Sea, a school that fell under their regional jurisdiction two hours away in Astoria. The archdiocese was cleaning house, refining their focus, working to save money. This is how they wanted education to work: in a streamlined, clean way. How they wanted boys and girls and women to work. Not like birth, or life: not a jumble of possibilities grown out of raw material. They first saw an opportunity at Star of the Sea when Jerry the maintenance man retired. They cleared out the rooms where he had kept spools and buttons, old record players and posters like the one of St. Francis of Assisi, the words *Walk beside me and be my friend* in bold Italian script on the door to the cave of reclaimed stuff where for years the children had gone for their craft supplies. The diocese public position was that Jerry's rooms were a fire hazard, that all these things were too messy, that teachers should just order classroom supplies from the catalog each spring.

As is the case for many children, my mother was my first teacher. Early on, her presence felt nearly omniscient, divine—at the very least, she was always nearby as a guide, and though she'd been raised Catholic, the spiritual tenet that carried forward into parenting was stewardship of the earth. But I was a freshman in high school, fourteen, by the time my mother began her first formal position as an educator, teaching at Star of the Sea. There, she immediately befriended Jerry and his burrow of basement rooms. I loved Jerry's rooms. They had that magic feel, I could have entered them through a garden or a series of earthen tunnels: never fully lit, always a sensation of dust even if you couldn't find it. Like my mother, Jerry was meticulous. He arranged his treasures in narrow rectangular boxes like government cheese used to come in, glued relics to the fronts so each box became a drawer displaying its contents as pull-knob. The boxes lined shelves around one small room; a thousand paper clips in one, a hundred fuzzy fabric balls in another. The drawers stretched from floor to ceiling, covered four walls. The very nature of this collection was often the source of inspiration for craft projects. I think of these rooms like vaults of words for magnetic poetry: The ideas come *from* the materials.

You don't think of a project and then go find the things to make it; you find the things that will shape the syntax of your art.

Another room was full of paper, stacks and stacks of flecked and colored and patterned paper, even sample wallpaper squares Jerry folded into small gift boxes. This was my favorite room. Jerry told me I could have whatever paper I wanted, and I took small stacks, giving silent thanks to the gods of fiber. I used it only for my best projects: small books of poetry, paper for the cardboard walls of dollhouses. I stored the rest in a cabinet and arranged and rearranged it, delighting in the textures against my fingers.

Going to Jerry's rooms felt like a field trip for the school's students too. My mother, whose classroom pedagogy rooted into inquiry and discovery, took her group of students there to acquire supplies. My mother's projects included soil study (she set up a table in her classroom where students brought in vials of soil from their various homes: sandy soil, loam, rich humus, forest floor compost, rocky soil, silt, silty clay, and so on), a backyard garden and worm bin (at one of the school's annual auctions, they sold a worm bin set, complete with student-narrated video instructions on how to operate it), the biosphere of a fish tank, and countless other projects involving close study of the earth. My mother loved small details, taught her students about these things. She called Jerry's rooms "the heart of the school." It's easy to picture each as a chamber. My mother believed that when they cleaned out the rooms, they scoured the flesh of that heart.

For seven years I taught at the Jesuit university, which claimed its roots in social justice, and I never attended Mass, never set foot in the chapel where daily they come up the steps like ants in their black overcoats to consider the truth, their mouths heavy with things to contribute. My classroom brimmed with students sweet as I imagine my mother at eighteen: she wanted good in the world, yearned for that grace her generation learned to seek in music and stones and candles, rows of grown-ups singing their hallelujahs into the pink, speckled dawn.

I came in from the garden dirty, papery skins of the plants clinging to my corduroys like offspring. I wanted to tell my mother about the way the light didn't fall through the leaves, it *leapt*, the way it lit the earth in its leaping, like a trout's shadow makes the water blush when the fish arcs for mayflies, drops of river full of color and sun making a second tail behind its first, but I didn't have the words for that yet. I'm not sure I have them now. My mother was probably doing some domestic job, something like kneading bread, probably wanted me to put my hands in it, feel it spring back against my skin. I can't be sure of every detail of memory: this could be why my name had boomed across the grass to me. My mother already knew about communion, about the ways we feed the soul. She'd seen the light through leaves a thousand times. She'd come west for this light, fractured and messy, and she was intentional in letting that light lead her children.

"Walk beside me and be my friend," those words I believed to be St. Francis, I learn from a Google search, are really from Albert Camus, a man I didn't know of until graduate school. I puzzle over his legacy. That he fought against nihilism seems appropriate. I carried his lines in my head through high school, believing in their power to strengthen community and true friendship by taking away the desire to lead and the desire to follow. The years a girl spends seeking truth can be her most painful, her most beautiful, best years. Jerry, I figured, knew what he was doing. He was organized; he had a shop full of records and tools, music and metal. He was like a blend of my father's tinkering, manual ways and my mother's carefully optimistic idealism. And he was also something else for me—a magician.

When they cleared out Jerry's rooms, they sold most of his things in the auction. I wasn't there, but I imagine the gym was full of dragons with their glittery scaled wings, record players with needles moving of their own accord, wooden toys talking, and children tapping their feet to a tune most grown-ups couldn't hear. My mother said they made a few thousand dollars on Jerry's things, turned the rooms into places to store uniforms, hold music practice. My mother is sad when she tells me they plan to close the school. A year and a half after her surgery, she still feels the effects of the growth hormone, and she's developed cervical stenosis, so her neck always hurts. She fears dying of an enlarged heart; she is sorry she can't visit more.

The winter snow has melted early in Spokane. Birds are saying things about spring—though I'm not sure if I believe them—and I've been thinking about the garden, antsy for the semester to end in May so I can put my shovel in the dirt. It's almost soft now. I take my daughter out and she stands by the strawberry bed, points to the canes of raspberries and peers into the worm bin. We have a lot to do out here. But the next day I must head to campus. I have some papers to grade, some students to meet. I'm still trying to figure out how to negotiate this Catholic system and show them how to walk inside of language, inside of light.

Jerry is in California now, pruning his roses and wandering his apartment complex looking for abandoned grocery carts he wheels back to the store on his walks. He writes to my mother and me on paper he's saved half his life, scraps donated to his collection from stationery stores in downtown Astoria. He sends us photographs of walnut trees, flowers, his happy face as he holds his grandchildren, yellow leaves covering the pavements' gray. He sends me scripture and prayers on cards of Mary praying. These are tucked inside the envelopes with the letters, not mentioned in his notes. He writes things like "I sure do miss your mother. She must be loving that daughter of yours." But my mother doesn't visit often. We're so far away from each other. I sure do miss her too.

When I was six years old, I grew curious about Catholicism, the religion that tethered my mother to her childhood, the large churches, the pretty dresses she wore. We lived in Des Moines, where her childhood church was, so I asked her to take me to Mass. The towering stained-glass windows gave off a feeling of hundreds of years of holiness, and even if it was just art and architecture, I walked softly, reverently. In the pews, we knelt and palmed hymnals that held the binding, glue scents of their age, and the words—pew, kneel, hymnal—all hummed like prayers on my tongue. The choir lifting their voices to the high arched ceiling also lifted me. I wasn't into Jesus hanging painfully from his nails, but I did find the lacy accoutrements something to linger over. I thanked my mother for taking me and tucked away the experience in a mind-file called Things That Shaped My Mother.

And, though I am not Catholic, I wonder: Tomorrow, will I walk over during one of my little lulls in a harried day? Will I ascend the steps, pull open the heavy doors? And if I do, will I hear my shoes walking together, their airy echoes in the nave? I wonder, briefly, if I will find my mother there, walking beside me.

But I know I will not.

Instead, I will look for a different place to work—where I can be my strange, blasphemous, mother-artist-professional self, questioning more than believing, asking my students to question, too, and to doubt.

THREE

LANDSCAPE ANXIETY

John Gardner says there are two plots: man goes on a journey, and a stranger comes to town.

In Ellensburg, I'm doing both.

I took the job because I needed it. I needed something that answered who I was, not a Catholic school that made me feel like I was using up a man's space, or a woman's who has chosen not to have children, or a woman's who had her children and raised them and then went back to work. I was thirty-six and had been mothering for so long—not so long as some, but the years had stretched and I was often alone with them; I was hungry to write and to teach poetry full time. (Also, we needed the money. That's a different essay, but it's also true.) I called my job talk "How Can You Not Want Me," after the opening lines of Melissa Kwasny's poem "Tobacco," but also I meant it, and if they didn't (want me), I'd walk away and do something else, where they did (want me). I was sick of apologizing my way around a toxic workspace. I had, as the youths say, No Fucks Left to Give.

It was April, and windy, the breeze pollen-full, and I ran up the hill to "survey my new domain" the morning of my interview. Below me, the rodeo grounds and the town and the university, its enchanting brick buildings amid the new spring fruit trees, their white blossoms blossoming into the pinked air, and beyond, the windmills and hills, and the snow-crested Cascades beyond that. It was, in short, charming. I ran back to the dorm-style-hotel where they'd lodged me and wrote a poem about some antlers I'd seen poking from a tarp in the back of a truck bed. They were attached to a head, and the corpse of an elk, under the tarp. They were on their way to be turned to taxidermy—I know because I asked the man when he came back to his vehicle at the truck stop. I thought taxidermy and tumbleweeds and sage and the rising moon the evening before the interview were all signs. This must be my new life. The pollen-air, not the taxidermy. I hoped.

*

Sometimes when I'm out walking at night under the full moon, the air smelling of sugar-tart apricots during fruit set—what they call the developmental stage between flower and fruit—and peach blossoms and the crabapple that swells the air in May, I like to steal people's lilacs from their yards. I walk up, clip the stem just above a new branch-bud, and walk away, my arms bouquet-full. I know my past is showing. I know it makes it seem I would take anything that smelled so sweet.

*

Before I take the job, my husband writes to Brigit Pegeen Kelly. This will be the singular most thoughtful gift he ever attempts. He tells her he'd like to purchase a broadside for my new office wall. He tells her she's my favorite poet. "I'm sorry," she responds, "I actually don't have any autographed broadsides or posters. (I'm afraid I have succeeded in trying to be invisible most of the time!)"

To be invisible most of the time.

It's how I'd felt for sixteen years. But his gesture is kind and almost knowing. It's one of the times in my marriage I felt briefly understood. Then he says, to me, "How sad, to succeed in being invisible."

And I know he does not understand at all.

*

I first learned to love the desert through Byrd Baylor's book for children, *Everybody Needs a Rock*. Peter Parnall's images and Baylor's words work together to tell us the rules. "If you can," she says, "go to a mountain made out of nothing but a hundred million small shiny beautiful roundish rocks." But the pictures show a person looking very closely at minute details on a very flat landscape.

It's similar in *The Desert Is Theirs* and *I'm in Charge of Celebrations*. I like the latter because the narrator invents her own holidays—like one for double rainbow day, one for the first day she sees a wolf.

"I keep a notebook and I write the date and then I write about the celebration," it says, right after saying it isn't lonely, out here, "in the deep ravines and the hawk nests in the cliffs," next to an image of a girl and her pen and the sparse grass, the cactus, the golden rock, and two large prints in the dust.

The landscape in the pictures picks up the myth of the story told so you can't tell if the myth came from the land or if the illustrations in these books came from the myth. I remember my mother reading them to me when I was a girl; I remember feeling like these books understood me, even if the author and illustrator were together in a very different place. Where I was, it was green—ferns, moss, ferns and moss on trees. Too thick to see far. You had to get to the beach or the field if you wanted a view. But the forest and moss were safe. And the creeks chunky and full of rocks.

*

My husband doesn't want to move to the small town. ("Just at first," he says, "until we know whether or not you like it. No need to uproot us all for a job when you can just commute.") So I commute. No one sees me do it. I succeed, for six hours a week, in being invisible. Like the land around me: sagebrush and basalt scablands and the invisible hawks and coyotes who call it home.

I spend six hours a week in my car in the high desert, Channeled Scablands, and several days a week in a town that's something between—a wide, wide valley, with a few deciduous trees surrounded by yellow hills, the mountains and ferns so far away.

It's a delight, actually. To be invisible for a while, in a different way than how I have been. No one sees me or needs me, but I see and feel. Invisible out here, where I'm so exposed.

Things I see, commuting the 180 miles, like half a circle, across yellow land:

A really burly man in a flatbed truck driving down through the gorge with a lily pot next to him. In my head, I tell myself stories of where he's going: To see his mother on her death bed. To visit his daughter in Montana. To surprise his loved one with something that would truly be a surprise.

Dogs. Hawks on poles and posts. Roadkill. Semis in ditches. Cars in ditches. Many, many patrol cars. The sky zipped to the land. The sky unzipped from the land. The sky gone light slate, like a dull painting. The scabbed lands yellowed, grayed, or all white. The feelings spread thin like cells across a glass plate, to examine under a microscope.

Things I feel on my drive:
Pulse-y.
Drifty.
Alone. *Deliciously* alone.

The small barn. *My* barn, at a specific milepost, where I know it's coming, out there in the middle of all those feelings.

I learn to process things. I have time I haven't known since childhood, time to feel and think and think and feel and process things. I begin to therapize myself during my drives, to dig out things I probably could have examined for years but never had time. I begin to look at things from my marriage, from recent years. Now I have my three hours each way. It's like long distance running but without the physical benefits or the exhaustion. It's just open space and open road. Driving it feels like being an early American. Or maybe a man. Ha.

*

I begin to speak into my phone, taking notes. Later, some make sense, or I make sense of them, and I turn them into essays or poems. Others don't:

In the middle of the night some of the birds are sleeping. I
slept like a bird without your arms, without a nest, without
a child. You can't make a birth plan there is no such thing.
You can't make a life plan either the grasses can't make
a plan in the middle of their lives they are green by the
end they are yellow which is more beautiful when the
snow falls.

In the rows of wheat that are shapes and spirals—

—the farmer has shaped his own brain—

—he has driven down into the wheat and thought of
himself as a mouse—

I don't mean mouse like rodent the kind your mother
screams and hits with the broom I mean the kind Leo
Leone meant when he wrote about them and their wall
and their colors and their paints and their imagining—

The telephone wires above me the trains to the right / one
yellow truck; I don't know what my beloveds are doing
right now

Or I listen to writing podcasts, like Kaveh Akbar talking about
resiliency and recovery and how his beloved lives in another place
than where he lives.

On the way to the town where I have no beloveds, I see two silos;
they might be water towers. I know what Richard Hugo would say,

full of "chorus girls and grain," coarse girls and green, I know what James Wright would say—to tear them down—

*

The first quarter I teach a poetry class, and things are going well, and then Trump is elected president, and Lucia Perillo dies, and Leonard Cohen dies, and Brigit Pegeen Kelly dies. I begin to wear black. That winter, away from my family for stretches too long to be away, I become deeply, nearly inconsolably depressed. I dream the world is ending. I wake sweaty and worried my children are dead.

Later that spring, I stop sleeping. I develop an insomnia so intense it becomes an anxiety so intense that it manifests itself creatively and in manic spurts. To manage it, I run.

*

For two years I drive back and forth, gathering the landscape in me like a new mother. All those cells that say open, empty, milky, or covered in white.

*

Sometimes I take the bus, to ease the drive. Also, to face some of what I've been processing during my drive—all the things I never had time to process while getting a degree and teaching and getting another degree and teaching and nursing a baby and working and diapering and working and friending and working and cooking and wifing and wifing and wifing and teaching and writing and feeding—

The bus swells like a wound about to open in me: I begin to experience recurring memories of the assault I experienced, on a

Greyhound bus, the summer I turned seventeen. I begin to associate things to other things—to have trauma nightmares, some in which my loved ones replace the man, repeat new, unexperienced assaults. It gets worse.

Then I beg my husband to move there so I can stop. I say, it's tearing me open into something un-fern-like. It's un-mossing me.

He cannot, will not understand. "Our lives are great like this," he says. "We love it here."

I drive back and forth until the end of the academic year. Then I break. I stop functioning.

Luckily, it's summer, the quarter is over, and I can rest. No one needs to know I am so tired. I can be invisible for a while. No one needs to know.

*

I spend large chunks of that summer in a hammock under a tree, watching the leaves. The bees. We planted wood ferns there years ago, and they frond up, knowing.

We eat fruit and attend art happenings. It's a way to go in public when I'm ready to go in public again.

We take our children to First Friday. One of the exhibits is a mutation show—based on cell growths in the body, it has a physical component, "mostly the colors of a valentine," says the six-year-old, "sounding like a melon in an elevator," he says. There's audio of the inside of a body too—like a heartbeat or moving blood, cycling through the chambers of the heart, ultrasound-ish.

They want to eat the suckers the lady is giving out. You can't have that, I tell my son. It has Red Dye #40 in it.

"Then I won't eat it either," says his sister.

Okay, I say. Just this once. And let's see how your tummy feels before you get in the car. I don't want you throwing up on the way home.

*

After the mutation show, my nine-year-old feels strange. She says the sound reminds her of something familiar she cannot quite remember, so it makes her feel empty.

In the car, I explain how in the womb you can hear your mother's heartbeat. You know where you are, but you don't. Your cells are floating around everywhere in her body. Your hair feces skin everything floating around, amniotic, then crossing the placenta, making her body a large dragon holding your small dragons.

So you might remember, I say. You might remember hearing my body from the inside.

"That makes sense," she says. "And it makes me feel better."

*

Driving across the state again, I feel strange. I feel something unfamiliar and something I cannot quite remember. I begin to think about how the landscape has to do with my anxiety. I develop a theory about it, beyond the bifurcated, double-residence life. I think it's the land out there.

I explain to a friend my theory of landscape anxiety—the drawing close we do when there are no trees. We make people into trees. We huddle, cleave, and cave. We get bunkered.

We seek our tree people, those with whom we would go into the ground, or fight off the apocalypse, or whatever people do when they have to face the end, and the world is too open. But in Ellensburg, I don't have a people. So I just work a lot and run a lot and feel a little unhinged.

*

When I was a girl, when we lived for a while in the farmhouse on fifty acres, my walls were patterned in crazy quilt paper I covered with posters of animals and pictures of animals from the magazines in the library free bin, hiding the wallpaper that was bright and wild, and once I developed a high fever and believed the animals in my posters were alive. I had figurines, too, everywhere, and I opened my eyes to see all the animals looking at me, furred, prowling. I couldn't tell if I was prey or part of a pack and who was who and whether I was human. I felt strange and I felt myself become part of the posters and part of the paper. My body pulsed. My fever held for weeks.

It was near this time that puberty began, and in my memory, they happen together. I found when I laid on my stomach, my preferred sleeping position, my nipples hurt—I didn't yet have breasts, but somehow, I could feel them coming, like dark bruises. I didn't even do anything fun to make them badges of honor. I hadn't climbed a dangerous tree or fallen down on a rock. I hadn't thrown my body against a door to break it down so we could see what was on the other side. Instead, I dreamed boys from my class were drilling me with dodgeballs over and over, to the chest. I had to ask a lion to shred the tough rubber. A herd of impalas to trample their sandwiches, their stupid rich bikes.

When I woke up, I was a different person. I felt like a stranger inside my own body. I had to go back to school.

*

In classics like *The Odyssey*, *Into the Wild*, and other famous stories about men, a journey happens over several years, with violent catharses and character revelations. Or a stranger comes and changes everything about the townspeople's lives, creating a paradigm shift, or several. We expect sex and/or love, and something that feels like a monumental arrival. In my story, a woman—raised unconventionally, now parenting two small children, married to a man who doesn't understand her but who once seemed like someday he might, who seemed borne from a family that might have portended security, who flatlined at capital mobility/being American—drives to another town, lives a solitary life of work and thought, and comes back every week, and nothing visible to the world really changes all at once. Her story is in the quiet in between. She just keeps going. But she's different inside from the parts of her she's heard and seen and laid out on the landscape, and the parts that are like an animal, killed and carved out and stuffed, and then bloomed back alive. She blooms them back. She knows this. No one else does. No one else even notices she died and kept driving. Kept making dinner.

She thinks maybe the best she can do is to document as much as she can in her own voice and see what sings.

*

Siri is Australian, and male, so he doesn't always understand what I'm saying. Either way he's a computer so he turns what I say into other language like we hope exquisite corpses or whisper games or other surrealist parlor tricks might. I say "I drove through a blizzard," and Siri writes "I drove through Bliss." Bliss is actually very far from what I drove through that night it took me twice as long to get from Ellensburg to Spokane, to my children, safely. For a while I am in snowdrifts a foot deep, my windshield iced over, my window down, my arm out to scrape off the building chunks so I can see to keep going.

I pull off at an exit ramp that hasn't been driven on since the storm began; my car barely makes it off onto the shoulder where I click on my flashers and get out, my boots filling with snow from the top in. I'm ready, though. I have a shovel and a sleeping bag in the back. And I'm already a ghost.

I scrape the ice off the windshield wiper and get back on the road. I'll crawl ten more miles, and it will take nearly an hour. I'm almost to the last hill before the city. I see the blue glow coming up through night, follow the blur of the red lights ahead of me, and hope for both of us that they stay on the road.

I'm almost to the end of this week's journey. I can hear my daughter rosin her violin bow in the warm room with the pine cones and jar of sticks we brought in from the river, smell the soup, the basil and tomato, simmering on the stove. The recipe is the one their mom left when she went to work years ago, among those she wrote out so they'd know how to make the things she made. Who was she then? And who is she now?

*

"The latter," wrote Gardner, "is the account of an invasion. It begins when the wanderer's shadow first darkens the doorway."

RUIN PORN

The poison hemlock in Port Townsend grows above my head. Its stalks are lovely, straight, and green, and it ends in a spray of flowers like Queen Anne's lace or cow parsnip, and if you didn't know how deadly it was, you might cut it for a vase, a homemade bouquet for someone you love.

I lean in to see a common brown snail climbing, the slime a glittery trail up the freckled path. Something's off. I push the snail shell with a stick of broken yarrow until it drops, hollow, to the grass below. I realize the snail dried up from the inside, became a ghost—a shell, a film of slime—clinging to the purple freckled stalk of the toxic plant.

Sometimes snails climb trees to escape their ground predators. Though it's dry in trees, there's still enough humidity for them to thrive upon, about 80 percent of that which is near the earth. And here, where the fog doesn't burn off until nearly noon, I imagine the woody stems are like Jack's beanstalk, something these little spirally gods might climb to their own sort of heaven. Except once they reach it, they die.

Are these snails trying to escape something and climbing the wrong staircase? Are they seeking ruin? Are they *being dramatic*?

*

I don't know what might correctly characterize those snails' imperatives on the poison hemlock, but I'm curious. I'm willing to investigate, to consider the relationship between snail and stalk, between wanting to escape a ground predator and knowing who exactly that is, between climbing into an attic or a barn loft or a tree to get away from the men below. Or climbing into a man's arms to escape another man.

In my experience, everywhere is danger. One must be wary. I also know what it means to draw toward certain forms of ruin, to love it, even, for its familiarity, its lack of pretense. I, too, have found comfort in a crumbled castle and a ghost barn, those that rot from the inside so the skeleton stands, useless, except for as the object of a photograph, or *a safe place for a girl*, wandering the fields, to hide from the downpouring rain, the thick shapes of men, walking through the fog, in the near dawn. I'm drawn back to these places, these ruins, because they form the imagistic, psychological core of me, but I also don't want them to become anyone else's porn. Take your camera elsewhere, part of me whispers, my eyes narrowed into scopes, spit forming on my tongue.

*

For a long time, I resisted writing about poverty because I didn't want to be anyone's Ruin in the Centerfold. I wrote around it, highlighting what to me was most important: my discomfort with financial privilege, my desire to retain aspects of my youth that were so advantageous to forming my foundational paradigms.

When I first wrote an essay about growing up in poverty and later living in an HOA, I tried to write against the arc of poverty to success, naming what I was and what I had been by depicting what I wasn't and would never be—writing that I *wasn't* unhoused as a child, despite not always having a permanent address, writing of my immense gratitude for natural spaces, my desire to share those spaces, to remain grounded, to not be carried away by capitalism or even by a set of shared community standards. That essay, "The Privilege Button," garnered a response from a wide variety of people—many who, coming from money, called it "eye-opening," and many others who, like me, sprouted from a lack of socioeconomic resources, found it "empowering." Several people contacted me to say it had given them permission to write about their own pasts. While I was and am grateful for these responses, I was also nervous when I embarked on a memoir of the same title—thinking I'd be able to write against stereotypes, against easily categorized notions of what "poverty" and "privilege" mean. But I could also tell that people interested in the memoir want(ed) me to participate in the easily packaged, dominant genre of poverty-to-privilege arc, of the story of the American dream.

Writing memoir is one way to take control of this story, and it's true that I'm more interested in being the subject than the object; the one with agency, who makes sense of the images, who creates the vision, rather than the one who is gazed upon. But also, I have no interest in participating in the trope that so many Hollywood film moguls and—more and more for a while there—New York publishers use. It's classist, racist, and sexist in ways I am zero percent interested in perpetuating. However, when I sit down to write, because I am writing about my life, and my life includes years in socioeconomic poverty, I must do so knowing the risk of commodification, of misrepresentation.

The genre is termed "poverty porn." It lenses on the "beauty of poverty," often oversimplifying, excerpting, and celebrating traits of those who live with less, materially but also less access to resources such as education and healthcare. And though poverty porn is more commonly applied through the romanticized gaze of the Western world on places such as those in India, Africa, and Central America, it's also more and more popular for Americans to turn that Othering gaze on their own communities: Appalachia, the Rust Belt, the rural Northwest—anywhere in rural America. But that gaze isn't comprehensive—it's a gaze, after all, not a nuanced knowing, and it often ignores systems of oppression, intersectionalities, and the Third World status the United States gives its own people as it fetishizes and further glorifies its own fetishizing of specific groups, or worse, additionally vilifies or makes caricatures of the members of those groups—buying into larger colonizer-as-savior or educated-elite-as-superior paradigms.

When writers get candid about their rural, impoverished roots, I get nervous. Back in 2017, I barely made it past page three of *Hillbilly Elegy* before slamming the book shut and tossing it in the giveaway pile. I almost threw it out the window! But I hang onto the occasionally contained self I've built on top of the also uncontained self, the one who would break something out of anger, whose child-self coping mechanisms involved outbursts of violence, things modeled for me and still inside me with which I cannot make peace or even fully recover, even as other parts of me think "don't throw that stupid book; it would cost a month's groceries to replace that window; you'll be cold all winter; don't be like your dad when he frightened you by throwing the chair through the pane, or the toaster across the kitchen—remember those coiled springs and your sorrow over no more toast? you're not the same desperate and angry ten-year-old who, in revenge and frustration, intentionally crashed your brother's radio down the stairs, watching it clank into so many metal and plastic parts, after he stabbed your doll through the chest with a screwdriver—"

Even as I write things like this, that to reticent me feels like maybe I'm selling out my childhood, revealing too much, oversimplifying it, excerpting it into true but out-of-context scenes—things that could possibly be seen as poverty porn, things that reveal my registers, my layers, my grammars and formative sociocultural responses—I have a system for checking myself. I send the writing to my sister, a UPS Store manager, who is incisive and smart and full of humor, and who lived through the same childhood. Well, almost. Not really. In her middle to high school years, our father was drinking less, and our parents had some cash flow to help when she needed things like pants for work and shoes for sports and band travel (and the flute that she played in band). My sister, though, is also sensitive, as one might put it, about revealing what to us feels private, what we were taught is private: our parents' lives, our family secrets. Not because we had anything to hide—though we did, like the illegal pot my dad smoked and the fact that he later drove without a license—but because we don't want to capitalize exploitatively on our de-capitalized, anti-societal upbringing.

Sending the work to my sister has another advantage too: she isn't An Academic, which I mean in the complimentary way—she's not caught up in any kind of discipline-specific terminology or buzzwords. She's influenced by larger culture but she isn't interested in appropriating or even critically examining the appropriation of what to us wasn't called "poverty," it was simply our life. And she is interested in the story and in portraying it with nuance and grace and realism—for an audience of people who didn't experience it.

This last part is what my sister points out to me when we discuss my work. She says, "Whether or not you want to write this stuff, people want to read it." And she tells me, "It might help them. It isn't porn if you don't make it porn. Just tell it like it is—the sad with the other stuff." It feels necessary to clarify that when she says "the sad," she doesn't mean poverty—she means the universally human experience of sadness, something we all feel, and in our case, we feel at times because we're made to regret not having things that allow us to participate in a capitalist culture, one that operates around material and money. Eating food from the garden isn't sad; however, when the volleyball team stops at a McDonald's on the way back from an away game, and your teammates all buy one dollar sundaes and you can't get one because you don't have a dollar and you don't really mind, but then someone says Ohhh why isn't she getting one?—then you maybe feel sad? Or do you feel sad because you wish the team wasn't choosing to reward themselves and bond with cheap non-ice-cream ice cream, and you don't yet know how to say that without being further ostracized? Or do you feel sad because when you finally get back to the school, the parking lot is dark, your father is way past drunk, no one can pick you up so you bum a ride home from a friend who lives near you on the back roads, even though her dad drove you home last time, and the time before, and it's beginning to put an awkward strain on your friendship? But isn't this what's sad, that I'm writing this human thing—every teenager has an awkward story. It's not original to feel left out or uncomfortable for one reason or another—but that in telling this, what I really fear is the reader who, in response, wants to give all children money for McDonald's, a corporation that benefits from our addiction to salt and fats, one that in turn benefits from preying on the next-to-poorest among us?

The answer, I want to tell this person, isn't buying us all McDonald's. It isn't a simple matter of material goods. The answer is changing the culture, the education system, the entire paradigm—or at least a team coach using her awareness, thinking about a wider variety of factors when she decides where to stop the bus on the two-hour, late-night drive home.

The answer is thinking more about our cultural differences, including a background or current life of "poverty" but also all the other ways we come at life differently and thinking more intentionally about the ways we interact with one another. And in order to do this, we need to be aware of those stories—not just as entertainment but as education. Thoughtful, textured portrayals—of a range of differences, large and small, across lives. Put another way by my friend Dawn, who grew up in a similar financial situation as my sister and me, "People always want to know someone who looks and is perceived to be like them, but carries scars." Dawn, working in academia by directing Evergreen College's Native Pathways Program, hits it on the head: it gives the reader consent to carry baggage too. It allows it space to exist—the Jungian shadow, the sister-self we banish to our subconscious. Reading about poverty, perhaps, elicits so many responses in the reader: visceral, vicarious gaze; pride in not having to experience it; empathy; desire to save; permission to exist fully. So there's a healing impulse here, akin to why we share any story—to create community around it, to increase empathy. Fine. Except . . .

I don't want sympathy. My life is, and was, just fine. (Or it was, as I wrote this. Later, it will be Not Fine. Then fine again. Etc.)

Like anyone's life. And some of my pain is connected, perhaps, to traumas I experienced, some because of random chance, and some, maybe, because of poverty—because of the systems it creates, the opportunities for hurting people, especially women. For a long time I feared facing and writing those parts; I feared making them public, like so many who grew up with visible vulnerabilities they had to hide in order to function in a society that stigmatizes and punishes the individual for their vulnerabilities. In order to make it, you fake it. So we cover them up.

My sister says to go ahead, write it into the work. And she means the essays in which I talk about the scary parts of marrying someone whose nuclear family is so Mainstream America/different from my own, the anxiety I've experienced while trying to navigate the hypocrisies of their worlds, to communicate with people who can't seem to hear me, or, as a child, Peeing in the Bucket because we had no indoor plumbing (to help us feel better about using a bucket when it was too cold to walk to the outhouse, my mother sang, to the tune of Sesame Street's "C is for Cookie," a song: "Pee in the Bucket/ is good enough for me"). But then also making clear that it isn't a big deal—we were kids, and lots of people in rural areas don't have plumbing. So not transcendence porn—no, this isn't that kind of story, either, even if it's also true: Kid from a House with No Plumbing Becomes Tenured Academic.

I've spent my adult life passing as middle class, blending in (if not fitting in), keeping a low profile about my roots, my (perceived?)

vulnerabilities, because I know what happens when people think they understand you—you surrender some of your authority. You no longer control where the camera pans, where it zooms in.

When I apply my own gaze to my experiences, I don't look down on them. I don't see myself as transcendent now; I see myself living another version of my life. And I see my sister—who decided college wasn't for her, and went on to manage five UPS Stores—as equally successful. Maybe more so, if we want to get technical, or apply salary range to the definition of "success." She makes about $20,000 more than I do, and she gets holiday bonuses and paid vacations. I use my "breaks" from teaching to catch up on writing, curriculum work, and grant-seeking for my department's reading series, as well as advising and mentoring students toward professionalizing—graduate school applications, internships, publishing, etcetera. Anyone in academia knows the month of December—"our time off"—is for writing twenty-plus letters of recommendation (and, if you're tenured, reviewing colleagues' tenure dossiers, writing letters for people going up for awards or promotions, or reading applications by people so overqualified you wonder how you got your job, anyway). For working with those students for whom you said yes to finishing the quarter on an incomplete, because of a variety of factors—lack of access, identity, health, poverty—that changed their chances of making it in the existing system. You understand these students on some level; you help them navigate. Invisible labor, they call this. But I digress. I was talking about gaze and self-management, self-protection.

*

In working on a memoir, I struggled to nail down what, exactly, my point was, my character arc/arrival. I realized I wanted to write into something new by writing against other things, the way we often teach students to approach composition essays. So I'm writing against traditional narrative structures, against assumptions about what a memoir is and does, against the expectation of capitalism-as-solution or success-as-arrival and against poverty porn. I'm writing against slumming as a form of tourism, against the depiction of rural America as piles of junked cars or the aftereffects of generations of societal neglect and socioeconomic struggle. That image of rural America is a façade; it's what the viewer decides to see. It's ruin porn. It's holier-than-thou porn. It's Ruin in the Centerfold, tuck-the-magazine-under-your-bed shame.

But . . . it gets complicated when the ruins begin to overlap and accrue, when you can't quite delineate them into entities, when you can't categorize them within yourself, when they resist classification. I know beautiful ruin: my uncle's house a patchwork of windows salvaged from junked cars and his chicken coop the shell of a Volkswagen van. And I know what it means to pull things from an old shed on someone else's property and turn them into practical household items. And I know it's trendy now: recycled art, junk deco, what the '90s film *Zoolander* hilariously homage-parodied as Derelicte. Trash couture. It's eco-friendly; it's cool.

And I know physical ruin: the bathtub full of flood silt, falling through the floor of the rental farmhouse, the old boat on blocks turned into a club house.

But there's another ruin that's more difficult to place: when two fifteen-year-old girls are left unsupervised and one of their "uncles" (a family friend close enough to feel like family) makes a move on them both. *Look at these innocent horse girls bred for my midlife crisis.* It's complicated—is it ruin porn?

And, thinks the part of me that's still a product of this American culture, this self-sexism, haven't I always tempted ruin? It's in my almost-immigrant blood, the portion of self that isn't native to this land, that knows there is a cellular, cultural disjunctive keeping me from being what the primal, unfiltered part of me thought my child-self was—of this soil, part of the web of watershed; not the pastoral but the born-into, one-with. No, I'm more like the naturalized plants—those that come in and make it a home, that root and bear new shoots. I'm the new shoots. I don't know anything before this, but as it turns out, I might be complicit in the ruin.

*

I'm going to try to tell a few ruins as they are, without adding lace or artifice. I'll just leave them in the margins, not put them in the middle of the stapled seam.

In the salal and western hemlock (tree, not poisonous stalk—see how closely ruin resembles grace?) that surrounded our home, several junked cars imagined themselves still fully metal, un-oxidized. They came in on tow ropes and cables, winched from the highways and back roads, my dad yelling in the rain.

Or where I was born: a gas station, upstairs, a chainsawed hole in the floor letting the woodstove's alder-cedar heat up into the space where my mother nursed me, the forest and ocean's ions wafting in the window along with the gasoline fumes and the clucks of chickens. Marijuana blurring the wild into the domestic.

Or back in the barn, the rafters swinging down their long arms to meet me where I climbed the mushroomed hay, my legs cut up from grass and thistle and blackberry, my hair tangled and full of field-stubble, the exploding fecundity of post-flood treasures, and like its own grotesque fireworks blossoming my brain, a dead cow replaying again in my mind, bloated, until, watching the filmy, fly-eaten eye, the distended belly and the legs stiff as a lollipop stem beneath a cake pop top, how I had poked that beast with a stick, afraid it would explode on my face, hoping it would.

Sometimes I wonder what exactly made me, what combination of flourish and rot.

Sometimes I dream myself back in the rental house we lived in on those fifty acres of floodplain, with the floor falling through in the bathroom so the tub had faulty drainage and backed up with silt during the high water, when the river welled up and the house turned to Ark Full of Loam.

Those who are from a place don't see the scenery—or the people—the same way the external viewer does. I lived a portion of my childhood in southwest Washington, land historically inhabited by Kathlamet people, a Chinook tribe, and later a Finnish settlement of logging and farming, now listed on the National Register of Historic Places for its covered bridge, often depicted as a "scenic drive." I remember playing in the river there, one of our swimming holes, where a rope hung from the underbelly of the bridge, swung out from the cement into the shaded water, the smell of tar and heat and then the splash when we hit the surface, and submerged, swimming to shore and then emerging, dripping, sun through the droplets, to see that rare tourist who turned off State Route 4 on their way to the coast to ogle the charming architecture, walking the gravel pull-out, and watching us splash and kick and crawl up the blackberry banks. The tourists smiling like they were on a movie set, at us, the extras, convenient local kids cast in the roles of playing ourselves.

But that pastoral, covered-bridge community you might see a glimpse of in real life as it appears also in tourism materials is not how everyone lived it. The camera doesn't pan back in time before Captain Gray, nor in panning forward does it pause on what matters to the girl living among those fields and roads in the 1990s—it doesn't offer a nuanced portrait of even the now. In a lot of rural porn, you get pastoralism or poverty. But what's real is, of course, somewhere in between. And neither, not both. As my sister says, "the sad [complicated] with the other stuff." The other stuff, and the sad, too, is complicated.

*

In my teenage mind, it was easy to associate from one known thing to another—the poison stalk, the desire to climb, or the twisted stair, the curiosity of descent. How easily I believed I was complicit in what happened to me. How the story turns, like a kaleidoscope, shapes that are both beautiful and unclear.

*

When I was thirteen, living in a rental house in Wahkiakum County, I found stacks of skin mags in the subfloor. A crack at the bottom of the wall left a gap, where the paneling didn't meet the floorboards, and I had dropped a necklace in there, so I laid down on my belly—and my newly budding breasts—to fish it out. I reached in, afraid of what living or dead animal I might touch. (I liked to stare death in the face rather than guess what it was, like some Halloween experiment, the peeled-grape eyes or spaghetti brains in the bowl.) My hand met something like books—no, like *National Geographic*, and thrilled that I might get some new pictures of panthers or underwaterscapes, I pulled out handfuls of magazines. There were about a dozen or more—*Hustler, Playboy*, a few others I can't recall. I read them and learned a lot about sex and the male gaze, not knowing that's what it was called, but I also read some very interesting literary fiction. I was thrilled mostly with the new experiences of language but also interested in how a woman would sit, her legs sprawled, showing us that pink series of labial folds and her unhidden vagina, a pose I found both vulgar and brave.

Whenever I ran out of library materials, I'd revisit the magazines in the floor. I even grew attached to a few of them, their stories forming the ways I saw the world. I must have read them all cover to cover by the time we left that rental, two years later, my body having learned its own patterns of blood and beginning to feel more than budding desire, more than simple curiosity at what was described so vividly in print. But I was still a girl, and the magazines adult material. Not wanting to get caught having read them, I simply left the pile where I'd discovered them, like a feature of the house that came preinstalled—woodstove, refrigerator, pornography.

After my family moved out, and my best friend's divorced father and younger brothers moved in (rentals are few in rural communities like ours), the youngest brother happened upon the glossy trove beneath the wall, and the family decided that they'd been right about me all along: I had been a perverted middle schooler and now I must be an even pervier high schooler. I was a "sinful whore who needed to repent" and their (Christian) daughter was not going to be spending time with me, not if they could help it. I didn't bother to correct them. Who was I to turn their gaze? And my young mind wondered, *Hadn't I read the mags? Wasn't I bad? Or wasn't I at least exactly who they thought I was?* It was 1995; I'd been to church and I'd been to school and I'd been to enough fishing docks and logging shows and county fairs to know there were only a few options. We didn't have the internet or sex-positive education. We had rural role modeling, the whore-Madonna complex, implied in the conversations men had about women, and women had about those of us who didn't come back to church. I wasn't a very committed Christian, so I must be a whore, or would be later on. I shrugged. Having read *The Scarlet Letter,* I knew I didn't believe in binaries—I just didn't know yet how to fully call out the pitfalls of hypocrisy and righteously cast shame.

Later, fleeing an abusive stepmom, their daughter and I stole her father's car and hid out in the attic of a house while the police lights flashed red and blue outside, strobing the night, saying *that sort-of-whore* (virgin-me) *and her not-a-whore friend* (virgin-her) *are up there, just beyond the crumbling carpet stairs, and they're aware of what they can do to men to ruin them.*

*

Of what men could do to them.

*

Of what it means to be fifteen and considered a whore when you are really a victim of a culture, of pastoralism, of a man—that friend's family friend—in his thirties, of his midlife crisis, or his lack of ethics, how complicated it is when he gets to know you, how he acts silly and fun—horse rides, paint wars, practical jokes—until you trust him, is the one who kisses you, when you say quietly, "I'm not on birth control; I've never had sex," and he says, "Don't worry, I'm not going to get you pregnant, I just want to teach you how to kiss," when he writes you letters for over a year after this, paying close attention, never going beyond that, and you trust him, so that when you ride the Greyhound a year later, and another man close to his age approaches you, you're used to being treated as if you're still being groomed; you don't know what "tease" means; after all, the family friend/uncle/trusted-person only kissed you twice, after months of joking and talking and paying attention; so this man on the bus just wants to be your friend.

Men in their mid- to late thirties and forties, you learn very young, are scared (of mortality? of absence?) and will find anyone who looks vulnerable. There is a certain type of girl-woman on whom they prey. The kind that looks like she hides porn magazines in her floor. She is aware of sex, curious about pleasure, she's hiding it poorly, she wants to learn. That man knows to say, "My favorite music artist is Sting" ("Don't stand so close to me"—you know it?—as he moves across the aisle to her seat, so she can hear him better), to say "Ti Si Glupa," to say "Don't worry, I'm a teacher," to ask what she thinks of his country, his language. This man imagines she wants it until he believes she wants it. She wants it bad in her sweet flowered dress and her strappy sandals. She wants it bad in her little denim jacket, embroidery on the pockets. She wants it bad when she falls asleep. Reading her novels and writing in her journal and listening to her Discman. Looking out the window coyly when he smiles.

*

I thought it was my fault, so I didn't tell anyone.

I didn't tell anyone about my friend's family friend either because *nothing really happened*. And he was kind. And he kept writing to me when he left town, so clearly, we were friends. I could be cool. But when his letters gave me instructions for what to do and where to meet him when I turned eighteen, I stopped writing back.

I didn't tell anyone about the man on the bus, because hadn't I talked to him, all day? Hadn't I listened to him talk, about Croatia and his travels and his music? Hadn't I been interested in the conversation?

*

Didn't I "ask for it," poking the dead cow with a stick, for the entrails and maggots?

*

I learned to shy away from men, from showing anyone the cars and barn and the field and rust and history. To only be curious when alone, to keep curiosity and textured shadow hidden under an aura of Knowing and Not Needing Help.

I learned that poison hemlock isn't safe for snails—even their thick, anti-toxin mucus membrane can't save them. They should have stayed on the ground, or crawled up something else.

*

What else I learned is that I can't protect other people, or animals, from pain. But I can say anything I want on the safety of a page, in the middle as well as in the margins. And that your own story isn't porn if you are the one telling it. That your story—every story—defies tidy charts and people driving through. It doesn't have to be easily pinned down or up.

There isn't one right way to share a narrative—there isn't one narrative, and what looks like ruin might be metamorphosis, and what looks like success might be suffering, and what looks like a settled life might be, well—might not be any of our business. As a writing professor, I tell my students we can choose which parts to share, and we can share them in our own shapes. We can mesh different things together and think about them in new ways each time. In doing so, we invent something revelatory, something that survives.

THE METAMORPHOSIS

> To dream
> you are bitten by a spider reveals a conflict
> with your mother. To dream of a snail
>
> suggests a spiraling inward for answers.
> —ROSALIE MOFFET

I. The Metamorphosis

For days after I read *The Metamorphosis* I kept thinking about the slow transformation. What did it mean not to dream you become a many-legged unfinished creature but to actually turn into a many-legged unfinished creature? I sort of thought Gregor would transform—into an actual moth, maybe, or even back into a man. Not just a dry, deflated, dusty, and weak-legged corpse with a rotting apple in its back. I sort of expected more.

Where I live there are more pine trees out my window than I can count. If the earth were an insect lying on its back, it would be a centipede, or maybe a billionpede. I would like to say I can see fourteen and make out the ridges of bark in their very straight trunks, but it depends on the angle at which I sit on the couch. If I am nearer the piano, I can see the ones in David's and Jerry's and Akbar's yards; if I am nearer the bird lamp, I mostly see the Wests' and the Schaffers', the one of the family whose house burned down two weeks before we moved in to ours. For the first year, the lot sat empty except for the concrete foundation, and we would take our children over to peer down and think about what it might be like if we weren't so lucky: if our house had been the one that burned down and we had to live somewhere while the father phoned insurance and the mom took the dog for a walk and taught yoga and Pilates and kept looking OK as if everything was fine even though all the family photos and the room where the baby learned to walk were completely erased because the chimney had needed one more inspection before Christmas Eve. They went to bed and woke up to flames everywhere, and they had to evacuate into the night.

I love our neighbors, and this isn't about them. It might be about our neighborhood, or any grouping of people, the lives we are all privately living. I thought about Gregor Samsa a lot because he was named, and he was taking care of everyone, had dreams for them even, wanted to send his sister to music school, and by the end of the story seemed totally erased. Just a night of crawling out to hear her play and then back to his room and bang, dead.

The pines don't have branches at the bottoms of their trunks. This is the way pines work; their lower branches often die. When the pine is short, it uses its energy to get tall, and parts of it expire. I should look this up to see how true it is. I imagine that during the hot season it takes a lot of water to keep those branches at the top growing, so they run out of water to share with those below.

And in winter, when it snows, the branches hold the white load and lean down onto the branch below, until they're a whole Yertle the Turtle stack of branches that looks as if the beneathest one is bearing all the weight. Poor Yertle. I understand the bearing of weight—I bear my own, all the past Mayas layered on top of the one who is the main character. The named one. The one suddenly weighted and weighed and corpsed.

When I woke one morning unable to go to work and speaking a language garbled and slow and losing its ability to be heard, I was not a long brown insect with tiny legs, I was not hiding under a couch. I was not a turtle, even. I was just more human. I had been to Alaska and had come back from Alaska, and my daughter kept playing "Lavender's Blue" on the piano, and when I looked up at the art strung above me on a line—clothespins, child's hands, snow person, collage—I felt like there was nothing left to say. I had had dreams; I had dreamed them, and now I was snowing all over inside, I'd brought the glacier home and was growing more glacier. I was a blue yawn of ice. In July. *Christmas in July*, like a used car sale, I laughed to myself. I would soon have to make a video for my students, introducing the summer poetry writing course, but I wasn't sure how to look at a computer or even make sentences, let alone talk about line breaks, units of sound.

Maybe what happened to me is what they used to call a "nervous breakdown." The medical world doesn't use that term anymore, and I didn't get a diagnosis. But my functioning did slip from top form for a few weeks. I went to a therapist and asked him if he could help, and he said it depended on what I wanted. He handed me his sheet of what he does for different types of clients, and I wasn't on it.

When I looked up at him, he nodded at my expression and said, "It isn't going to work on you," as if he'd already resigned himself to me being impossible.

I had wanted someone to tell me I was possible, that my life would be possible.

We broke up after that.

Well, we broke up after the duende. I assigned him Lorca to read because when I was explaining how I saw the world and the issues I was having with my husband, he didn't understand. I didn't explain well enough that my husband refused to talk, would not engage in conversations about moving to where I worked, how difficult the commute had been, the bifurcated life, how I worked too hard and carried too much for our family. Instead I began with duende. He had said, "Fine, send the pdf," and so I did. And, because I had been to the H. J. Andrews Experimental Research Forest, I also explained the thirteen years that the spotted owls had left and the ways you could get close to them if you sat still in the forest for five hours. I explained how scientists track hummingbirds, by injecting a small chip in their necks then making a map of their flight patterns. And I explained how the heart of a blue whale is so large that strung up, like a suspended testicle, it is taller than a human man. All of these things, plus embodied cognition, I thought might begin to make clear why I was hurting so much. My therapist said he understood this but not the duende, and I said "I think we have to call it then. It isn't going to work with us."

To dream you are a human in a live body in a life that you cannot comprehend—years after you dreamed of one day being a human in a live body outside the small towns where your family rented houses—is to live a life in a body that your child body didn't imagine fully.

II. The Child Body

My child body didn't imagine a life exactly like this, but I'm not sure I had a clear picture of what this life would be either. It was hard to imagine things I hadn't seen an example of, hadn't known anyone to experience. Adult Maya was carrying so much—so much "success," so much "possibility" for her children—and had nowhere to put it down, no one to help her carry it. Child Maya would have run away to the barn, the river. No one in her house played musical instruments or traveled by airplane or went out to restaurants or ever gathered in groups as large as those I'd sit in during my first lecture hall course (in fact, the entire population of my high school was less than half that of my first college history class). When I went to university I did so with stubbornness and determination and probably the weight of duty (not unlike Gregor Samsa, compelled to work) but also a sense of disbelief that it was happening, after all those years of working and dreaming, because my initial dreams, after all, were larger and maybe more selfish than those of Gregor Samsa (I wanted, when I went to college, to live a life of less servitude). My brother had dropped out of high school his freshman year, and when I was admitted to the one school to which I'd applied, Western Washington University, he said "I guess you think you're some kind of big shot now." I didn't think I was a big shot in the way that he meant, but I did think so in terms of how I felt. I felt like I was on top of the pile of turtles, as well as being every turtle underneath, except all of the Mayas underneath could hold the rest of me up, and we were a strong and capable pile of turtles, and some of us pulled into our shells, but the rest beamed and waved and looked out across the fields to the horizon. We were completely unstoppable, even if—especially if—we didn't know where we were going.

Partway through my freshman year of college, I encountered a concept called graduate school. I didn't know what graduate school was, so when I heard people mention it, I thought it was another version of what we were already doing, except it was for people who had already graduated (which, for those reading who don't know, is called post-bac—but I didn't know that then). It didn't occur to me that I would need to go to graduate school or that I would even be capable. I had applied to the English Department and the School of Education because teaching literature and writing was a thing I'd seen respected adults do, and anyway, I'd been doing that since I could read—teaching my younger sister, my older brother, my classmates and friends, my stuffed animals—literature, and writing, and science, and all the things. Learning was easy. I loved learning and sharing curiosity and ways to spiral into new ideas. In school, I finished my work quickly, and sometimes, if the teacher let me, the assigned work for the remainder of the year (by October or November), and then I read or memorized poems and helped teach the class until school let out. Because we lived in rural areas with very small populations and educational opportunities, there was no such thing (except during one semester I attended Astoria High School) as Honors or Advanced Placement, so until I went to college I didn't really understand, nor had I encountered, many of the concepts that in college my peers already took for granted (among them, thesis statements).

My child body imagined a future filled with things like bookshelves and ceramic dishes and a quiet house with rugs and cats (think Disney's *Beauty and the Beast,* except no magical household items, and a much smaller house, not a castle). I knew "There must be more than this provincial life," but in my child body's imagined future, I don't think there were men—or at least not men who took me for granted, built their relaxed lives on my constant labor. Sometimes there were children, but they were small and quiet, like magical creatures or wild animals, and I was quiet, and adult life altogether was quiet. I didn't imagine it rollicky and busy with in-laws who were constantly judging me or obligations to socialize regularly with people whose worldviews were drastically different from my own, who expected me to fit into their paradigms or be trampled into nothingness. I know that was naïve.

When I lay on the floor that summer, looking up at the string of art and listening to my seven-year-old daughter play on the piano, I was thinking about whether or not I wanted the life I was in. It was difficult to understand how I'd arrived there. I knew—I mean, I'd made the choices—but I wasn't exactly sure how this was my life.

III. Thanksgiving

"You're always trying to sabotage the holidays," my husband says. His back to me. It's night, the covers over him. Outside the raccoons are making work of the fishpond. I keep my legs on my side of the bed so his toenails don't scratch me. He says, "You want to ruin everything."

It's not true, but I can see how it seems that way. Earlier, I walked into Thanksgiving at my in-laws' and there were probably forty people at several large tables. I had imagined it with fewer people—the invitation text had only four recipients, two couples—the sons and their partners. But there had been so many cars outside when I pulled up, I should have known. I was worried only about how late I was. Normally when they say "we'll eat at two" they mean 2:30. It was 2:15, but I'd stayed home an hour beyond my family's departure to finish our food contribution: marshmallow-free sweet potatoes and vegetable broth-stuffing for our meat-free children. I knew they would have no other vegetarian options (as my daughter used to say, "Mom, they put bacon in the salad"). I had planned to arrive on time and stay three hours.

Everyone looked up and greeted me, a bit aggressively, with smiles that felt put-on. Probably they were feeling kind and benevolent, like people who say "Are you new here?" every time you attend your own church, three times a year. But I could feel my too-warm coat. The oppressive smell of hot turkey. The glare of my mother-in-law, from under her smile. I immediately turned sweaty and nauseous. I found my children and kissed them on their heads, indicated where to find their special sweet potatoes and stuffing, and walked out the front door. I didn't know how to go back in, so I got in my car and drove away. I texted my husband: I'm so sorry. Love you.

I drove to a trail where I'd be able to get to the river. It was a mistake. The wind had blown down too many trees and the rest they'd cut. The trail was carnage. Charred-trunked ponderosas spilling off the basalt cliffs above. Like a pile of pixie sticks. Or turtles.

I made it to the river where I frightened two mallards—a pair. They swam out, quacking lightly, into the current. In summer I pass this spot in my kayak. It's always slow here.

I breathed in and out for an hour, trying to focus on the tall grass and the river's eddies. I knew it would be a problem later, this panic attack, but right now I just wanted to feel okay.

IV. To Dream of a Snail

I figured out the patterns of these panics—they happened in waves. It was during those years when I wanted so badly to have big conversations with my husband that he was simply unwilling to have, those years just before the pandemic, when I worked so much, was so overwhelmed that small annoyances grew into oppressive beasts: heat, crowds, noise, too much food, senseless (to me) adherence to traditions that prevent individuality, in-laws that didn't try to understand. For years, those in-laws judged every move I made: parenting solo when my husband left on another coaching trip; and when he lost his job, the fact of my taking a position in another town to save our mortgage, our home; leaving my children to do said job—the work that pays our bills; choosing not to feed my children fast food; seeking moments of solitude and silence to recover my mind, my body. And there are things I could do to lessen the feelings of anxiety: exercise, sleep, drink lots of water, eat vegetables, read, practice solitude, avoid in-laws. Hang out with people with whom I feel safe, can be real. Reading through this later, I realize I'm describing what millennials casually call self-care. But I learned that no one makes room for basic self-care in my life except me. I can't count on anyone else to notice my needs, *or even listen when I articulate them directly!*, and help me achieve them—I have to fight for that space. No one else is going to do that.

Not everyone understands anxiety; despite memes and other social education, it still carries a lot of negative stigmas. And I have many friends for whom this is a typical part of their daily lives. These are kind people, successful people, published authors and artists who make their livings from art and brainwork. But they don't often fit snugly into capitalist paradigms. They don't succeed in pretending we're all fine all the time. They don't "America" well. They do their work in the margins; they function highly, from the margins. They raise children and organize communities and manage creative endeavors. Like me, they're introverts, thinkers with the capability to perform a public persona, but only an authentic one. And like me, the world of pretending-to-be-happy-all-the-time isn't built for them.

Telling myself that other thinking people experience this, too, helps. But it also comes with a whole mess of other feelings.

My husband says, "Do you think being creative makes it worse? It's sort of weird that you and so many of your friends have this." He says he just tries "not to overthink things, that's why [he's] always okay."

My in-laws tell me I sure attend a lot of writer events. "You're always off with your friends," they say. "You miss a lot of family events for those things." I don't know how to explain to them (though I've said it plainly, directly) that everything I do publicly, for writing, is part of my career, my tenure application, my post-tenure review. Every travel on which I embark is for work. Even writing is work now—because it has a public/professional outcome. And that the family events feel like abusive spaces where I am constantly being strung and quartered—in my body, I feel them dissecting me, not to understand but to bleed me out, figuring out how to dismantle my corpse. How to corpse me.

My husband says, "I feel like you don't try at all."

I promise to try harder.

He says we've been getting along better. I don't tell him I've been burying myself again.

*

Sometimes, in the middle of a panic attack, or in the aftermath, I wonder if I am undergoing a very rapid transformation, the kind that almost happens overnight, the kind that happened to, say, the Imagist poet H.D., after Ezra Pound rejected her, after Freud's sexist psychology messed her up further, and then she sailed away with Bryher and became a happy person who didn't need men. Good for H.D.

As for me, at the "height of my powers," as my friend Ellen likes to jokingly say, my body could barely stay asleep or still; I would wake fevered with ideas, write surrealist stories at 2 a.m., wildly fill the pages of journals, go running at 4 or 5, floating spore-like over the terrain, for sometimes ten miles without noticing how far I was going but feeling empowered by the secret movements of wind and the waking sun and horses and trees and even the rocks under my soles. I became very lean and very physically strong, without trying. My mind—seeking escape from extended family, from middle-class America—was a constant burst of glittery curiosity. I felt like I spoke a hundred languages. I felt I could walk into a room and command all attention at once, if I wanted, like a heroine in a middle school movie. Friends asked what diet or regimen I was completing, and I'd laugh and say, "Just stress!" and change the subject. But after the wave and the crest and the crash, nothing really changed, other than my ability to fake contentment, even my ability to feel intensely. I guess I thought, how I thought of Gregor, that I'd become something—an actual winged creature, maybe, or even revert back into a teenager. Not just—to paraphrase my treatment of Kafka's character—a dry, deflated, dusty, and weak-legged woman approaching menopause, her two breasts reinflating to 36D after their brief stint as 34Bs. I guess I expected more than getting my breasts back.

What was it Gregor wanted? What is it I want? I'm more selfish than Gregor, more desiring, less patient with the outcomes of fate and my limited role in an oppressive marriage, the domestic space. Was he happy when he crawled out to listen to his sister play her music? That part broke my middle-aged heart. I remember vividly how I bawled when he shuffled out, so decrepit, just to hear her play and how it was enough for him, how he crawled back and died. I understand that the story is flawed—especially scientifically—I mean, c'mon, Kafka, he clings to the ceiling but then what? No liquefication and regenerating from the soup of enzymes and tissue and imaginal discs to become a reformed body? Maybe

Kafka didn't know that's what caterpillars do? Maybe he didn't understand about insect science?

Like lepidoptera (a butterfly), to embrace the cliché of metaphoric transformation, most of our genetic makeup is formed before hatching/birth—inside the egg of our genesis. So the emotional capacity of an adult woman is probably decided long before society gets ahold of her. She's probably carrying around eyes, legs, wings, and so on in her imaginal discs, dormant and unused. Once I read that some caterpillars move around the world with little "rudimentary" wings furled up in their bodies. Invisible, internal wings. I think about this—and caterpillar soup a lot, actually. Whenever I see a tween's bedroom or a tramp stamp or a caterpillar crawling on a leaf, I think oh, yeah, it has tiny unseen wings, like mythical Geryon or . . . like all of us. How do we get them to sprout? If an anxiety attack isn't enough to do it, is anything? (I don't know it yet, but I will need these wings, later.)

V. To dream / you are bitten by a spider

I never had a dream I was bitten by a spider, but I did dream many other things—ghosts and ancestors come to speak to me, the intellectual presence in moss or trees, a way of communication that involved speaking to inanimate objects. The subconscious world as a different version of our lives, a way to process what's happening on the surface. I thought of heightened consciousness, brought on by extreme stress and work, as akin to an orb weaver or the other animals that practice embodied cognition not just as a philosophical tenet (the body and mind influence one another, the mind is controlled by physical experiences of the body, related to Heidegger and Lakoff) but by praxis—the spider that stores thoughts in its web, the octopus that uses an arm as a penis and keeps memories and even received sperm in its tentacles or tucked somewhere else, for later. Perhaps, I figured, if those in my life didn't understand or want to discuss what else this life might look like, I would process in my sleep, my fiction, my imagination. I embarked on some intentional access to my subconscious-in-writing, to devote renewed fervor to marginalia, to value even more deeply my relationships with creative friends, with manuscripts—those I read and those I wrote, with art, with duende and the surreal.

Was this what H.D. meant, when she spoke of jellyfish consciousness? Was she meaning that the ways we experience the world might meld together so that our absolute creative and intellectual powers were aligned through sex and thinking as one? These are some of the things I was pondering as I dreamed in animal/magical realms. These are the things my husband did not want to discuss.

I wrote a Kafka imitation-riff in which an ant wakes to find he is Gregor Samsa. The story is silly and then turns a bit when the ant discovers his sexual organs. During that phase of my energies, I also held an extreme awareness—at all times—of my sexuality, my need to enact it (this part, as you might imagine if you know cis hetero men, was cool with my husband—those years were full of a lot of sex, one way he was willing to connect). I needed to experience the body fully and the mind fully and the emotional landscape fully, and I found nothing felt fully satiating or aligned, that I was trying and trying to enact a full experience but with limited capacity for merging my faculties, as if I was a species in the wrong body.

VI. The Inward Spiral

In the end of this period I was not quite Gregor (dead) but also not quite a butterfly (cliché)—I was something between death and beauty; I was still living the life I was before but carrying the dream of something else (mysterious) like the wings inside the caterpillar, except they will never emerge, and no one will ever know they are there. I thought. Or maybe I returned to the child-self, before she put on all those clothes that didn't fit, those layers of dullness she wore in order to pass as a human though inside she felt alien, felt alarm. I thought I'd emerge from my midlife metamorphosis able to understand and speak what others do, but instead, I thought to myself, I'm just still Maya, the dullest version of myself, no actual transformation into anything new at all.

What does a woman do when she isn't all the other turtles piled beneath anymore, but just the one on the bottom of the stack, the original turtle, Yertle, just hanging out in the pond?

As usual, she turns inward, into the self no one knows. The one on the couch, alone, watching the trees change again, thinking about the Fibonacci sequence, the slow snail moving across the lawn, toward the dormant rhizome of a fern or iris, the ones that grow along wetlands and ponds. She waits for something else to enact itself upon her, a rift that will pull those wings out, demand the turtles pile up again so she can launch off them into the creature she knows is still inside.

HOW TO TRESPASS

The first day of sixth grade Honors English, the teacher asked my daughter and her classmates to write about what it would be like if they could fly.

Or more precisely, the question was, *What if humans could fly?*

That's not a very original question, my daughter said. Nor does it really offer a very intense challenge, she said. I mean, we've been writing stuff like this since first grade.

In myth, art, science, and literature, flying has a history. Icarus isn't new, and neither are the Wright brothers, nor Amelia Earhart, even though the novelty has not worn off. What's new to say about flying?, we wondered.

And what's it teaching you about how to write? I added, but then I also noted it was probably an entry task, just to see where they were, skill-wise, what educators call a *diagnostic assessment*. What they wrote about, and how they wrote it, would give the teacher many insights. No one really cared what my daughter thought about humans flying.

Too bad.

***

They say flying dreams mean you feel free. And that falling dreams mean you are worried about something. I have had my share of both—both flying and falling as forms of trespassing into the sky, where a human doesn't belong, borrowing the idea of wings or the crash when we realize we aren't weightless but bound by rules like gravity, a force that pulls our greedy bodies back to earth. Back to reality.

But sometimes I imagine I am a bird, so I can fly over our neighborhood and see it from the aerial, forgetting for a bit the human part of human-animal. Other people might want to just use Google Earth, which you can also do, but I like to think about the smells and the sounds, which Google Earth doesn't have: the buttery-pine scent of the ponderosas when their sap warms in July. The squeals of children on bicycles and the screech of other raptors—I like to forget about being human. Let's say we're the bald eagles that live in the river valley to the northwest of those children's houses, past the richer people's houses—I fly past their wide yards and wide fields beyond, where I like to plummet down quickly for a mouse, or no, why waste time on a mouse when I have the whole winding river, its shady spots where trout dart and suckerfish troll the silty, crawdaddy bottoms. I wait until I see them near the shore, those shadowy, liquid forms in early morning or evening hours, when the insects those trout are after skim the water's surface. I dive through the caddisflies and mosquitoes to grasp a plump and speckled fish, and then I fly over everything, back to my tree, a post-lightning branch of an old cottonwood, to eat, tearing that pink meat for the fat of it, and sometimes, when I'm not careful, or I pause on the way home, I drop the fish in parts, by accident, in the fields or too-near the trail, so those scavenging coyotes or those out-wandering human children might find them, and ask their mother: "Why is there a fish in the field? Why?" Their mother smiles and explains us. She explains what they—the human children—can eat and what they cannot. She tells them how to avoid getting caught when they climb the fence from the Fish and Wildlife-designated terrain to that earth kept by the private landowners (boundary rules we eagles do not follow). She explains the rules of trespassing so that they know why their middle-class privilege in their middle-class home can also help them navigate what's slightly more wild but also slightly less public: these acres beyond. Where we are, where we return every year, make our nest, where we keep expanding our numbers. There are four of us now. There used to be two.

But I am not a bird. I am the human mother. Unlucky/so lucky. And I live in a house paid for by my education—or, by the results of it, *poetry*, and I'm grateful, and I'm also pulled daily by my wild stirrings to run or hike the trails that zigzag through public and private lands, up to Rattlesnake Ridge, on the other side of this valley. It doesn't seem like these boundaries should exist, and when I was a child, they didn't, to me, because none of the distinctions or patterns were ones that held me. I didn't see them as I do now. I went anywhere I wanted. I mapped land by where the rain fell and where it gathered and how it left again, and also by what plants I wanted to eat and which ones made good shelter if I wandered all day and got caught in the rain, and by which I could burn and by which belonged to each other, symbiotically, and to the animals who saw no borders other than the ones they themselves made in reaction to their needs and their fears, which is how people make lines: by fear and to feel like they belong.

I live in a neighborhood where several things belong: plants, animals, and people—the ones making the rules of what belongs. The ones I fear.

If you flew over us and beheld an aerial view (of these rules?), you'd see a 1970s plot map with non-identical houses punctuating an otherwise treed landscape, and down a slope to the northwest, the Little Spokane River winding through a lush, green valley, with fewer houses—mansions, really—surrounded by their false borders of green. These people are wealthy and want NO ONE in their spaces. They paid to put in a locked, coded iron gate at the top of their long black driveway, with bars that wrap around the sides and join to the fences of neighboring houses. To get in, you need a code. Or you need to be really small or able to fly.

I have one of these things, so I'm running down the road one day, having my solitary exercise on a route I enjoy because it's storybook gorgeous and quiet: maples, Douglas firs, snowberry, sword ferns, and moss to both sides, a natural spring gushing out of the hill to my right, and light streaming through the foliage to the left, fairy-like, my children say, and it's rare to see another human or even a car.

But a car—a Porsche—pulls up next to me now, and slows, and the driver leans out.

"Hey," he says, his brows narrowed, "What code did you use to enter the gate?" His golf polo blares its bleachy wealth in my face.

"The code," I answer calmly. "The code that was given to me."

"Are you visiting someone down here?" his wife asks.

"No," I say, "I'm just on a run."

The wife's face turns red. "This road is *not* public access," she says. "Who gave you that code?"

"Our neighborhood has access," I say, again, calmly, but with assertion. "Your neighborhood sought access to build the gate, so we gave you an easement—but it wasn't meant to be a private road, so we have the access code to the gate." I'm not completely sure that what I'm saying is true, but I like the way it sounds. Official. I figure they'll drive away and leave me alone. Most of my life I've pretended to have authority in order to be left alone—I figure this is one of those situations. Assert authority (I can pretend to be an eagle!), remain composed, don't give away your past, act like you belong. (I'm well aware this strategy only lands if I am using all the affects of formal language register to offset my shabby, rather less-than-elite-looking clothing.)

Usually, this set of rules—playing at the affect of privilege—works. This time, not so much.

"Whoever told you that," the wife states, coldly, "lied. We have legal paperwork showing that it's not—"

Here, her husband shifts his shoulders, cueing her to stop. It's his turn. He's going to set me straight as his . . . nine iron?

"We've had things stolen out of our garage," he says. "So this is not a public road. If you want to go down to the valley"—and here he has a look of disgust that people do this, access the valley adjacent to his Home—"just take the trail on the other side of the neighborhood—the one for your use." He says *your* like a movie villain might, like I am a cartoon rat, and he is the cartoon King.

I feel sorry for them both: Don't they know that the people who stole things from their rich, open garage stole them without having typed in a gate code? That the public access—at the other end of the beautiful, middle-class, treed neighborhood that runs the length of the ridge above the valley—is how those garage-stealers reached his coveted stuff?

I look at him and he looks at me and I shrug, saying "Well, I can do that next time, but I'm just here to go for a run. I'm not stealing things from your garage. I'm sorry that happened to you." He gives me a look that says, "I'm going to call my lawyer," and drives away.

I don't have a lawyer (how could I ever need a lawyer?) so I resume my run, the thrushsong conspiring along with me—"there is no gate, there is no rule, you have the code" they sing, sending me, too, the smells of nettle and ocean spray and mock orange, sending me their wingrustle leafcall—and I call my husband and say, "You may be getting some emails soon. Sorry. I sort of ... trespassed again. But I did it right this time—I used the code!"

My husband is, at this time, still HOA president, and he is the one who gave me the numbers: JFK's assassination date. (Whoever came up with the code has a sense of humor, I think to myself every time I type it in—JFK, an advocate for civil rights... and JFK, who himself wasn't perfect, a product of a nation that couldn't quite arrive in its own promises, a nation obsessed with ownership and access but not understanding stewardship or Indigenous sovereignty or . . .)

We both know this is one of those liminal trespasses, the kind for which I played my privilege card for access, not the kind that fifteen-year-old Maya might apply, a Maya who would have lived—if she was lucky—in one of the government-subsidized apartments down the street from us. Not those teens who possibly broke into this golf-club-joined man's garage and stole what? sealant? an oar? a tarp? What does a person bike down a half mile of gravelly switchbacks and then across half a mile of shaded blacktop steal? And how do they bring it back up the hill? I don't think anyone stole anything. I think he made it up. The teens riding their bikes down the trail are going down to smoke pot or swim or have sex or take senior pictures. They could care less about your rich garage, dude. Or maybe they did steal something, just for fun—who knows. I remember being a teen who needed to make mischief—who needed to do something so she didn't feel penned in by the artificial boundaries of social class. Who was always sick of the pointless, stupid rules.

* * *

When I was fifteen, I trespassed every day. I lived in a rental house on fifty acres, only one of which was part of our rental, the rest given over to hay and cows, also in a river valley; and I walked them and fished them and ate berries from them daily.

But those fifty acres weren't enough, quite; not for this far-flying bird. I also needed an orchard, where my brother didn't go, and

I needed a rocky bend of river where my parents didn't go, and I needed the old-growth forest land "owned" by Weyerhaeuser and the old barns owned by the hay and cow people across Wahkiakum County, and I needed the field of daffodils by the tiny glittering stream where my friend and I rode her horses, and where I recited Wordsworth (one of the only poets I knew then) to myself, and to her, and she said "Your head is so full of poems and dreams."

I had those, and I was glad to have the rocks and rivulets to say them to, because no one in school really cared about books in the same ways that I did. I certainly didn't have the option of Honors English in sixth grade and would have been thrilled to be asked to write about humans flying, and it wouldn't have occurred to me to think about how the writing might contain literary devices either—I didn't even know what they were (literary devices—techniques for writing, craft choices). I knew rhyme and meter and metaphor, sure, but I didn't think about things like *metonymy*, where you use something closely related to refer to the thing, or *synecdoche*, when you substitute a part of something to represent the thing itself—both of these types of metaphor. Metonymy: "lands belonging to the crown." Synecdoche: "I become a transparent eyeball," wrote Ralph Waldo Emerson. He had a "bird's-eye view" of the woods and world below him. He was capable of seeing so much because of . . . imagination? Access? Lack of oppression? Friends who spurred and encouraged his inquiry?

***

I think a lot about dreams and language and flying around like a transparent eyeball, actually. I think about land rights and taxes and access and who has it and who doesn't. I tell my daughter that Honors English will be better than non-Honors English always was, but I don't know if it will, and I don't know what better means either. A few weeks after the quarter begins, she says that her teacher is working hard to help them learn how to be organized, and though they aren't reading any books yet, they do have interesting discussions, in part because the other students in the class like to read and talk about what they are reading (rather than goofing off, my daughter doesn't say, but implies). And the other students in the class seem to live in or near our neighborhood. So, we've purchased our daughter access to peers who also love books? She has the code—she can go where she pleases. And exchange ideas. I can't help wondering what her demographic looks like, what that exchange can contain, in terms of life experiences. What price for what access.

* * *

When I was a freshman in college English, honors, and humanities courses, I always felt like I was trespassing on someone else's land. The rules were much the same: Act with confidence. Assert authority. Remain composed. Don't give away your past. Act like you belong. Don't tell them you have no idea what Ulysses was up to; you didn't read it in high school. Don't tell them, either, that you have your own ideas about and reactions to the literature you are reading together, that you feel the characters differently. That you don't always understand how any of the options on multiple choice are the correct answer, that you have to work hard to imagine yourself into the heads of those who made the tests, that it is easier to imagine yourself a bird or a fish, or an octopus. Sometimes

I felt like I was trespassing on *land that wasn't mine*, that perhaps I knew better than they did because I didn't see it as something I owned, I saw it as something that owned itself—as a friend, as a house I was visiting, as a whole neighborhood. Don't step on all the little houses, I wanted to say. Don't peer into their windows either—it's rude. I was passing through, I was paying attention in different ways. I was also aware I was still trespassing too.

***

The year my daughter begins sixth grade is the first fall of the COVID-19 pandemic, and most schools have remained virtual. Our school district, however, in a somewhat conservative corner of eastern Washington, in a county that swings red, politically, or is at least one of many deep purple bruises in an otherwise blue state, has elected to offer in-person classes, due to pressure from the district's families. So my daughter, fully masked and armed with her own vial of hand sanitizer, enters Honors English—and middle school altogether, for the first time—already aware that we live in a fear state. When she writes about flying, she writes about "humans not needing to take over and capitalize the atmosphere, too, except we already put a giant amount of chemicals into the sky as it is." Couldn't we just leave something alone, she says.

And in the second week of school (which is late September, delayed two weeks due to COVID safety preparations, then another week due to hazardous air quality from wildfires in the west—compounding the issues of indoor and outdoor air quality), the week Ruth Bader Ginsburg dies from cancer, and the nation braces for the 2020 election, school pictures are taken, and the administration and photographers offer students the option of removing their masks for the photo. My daughter relays that all the students elect to remove them, so the photographer—and grandparents sharing them, and future generations gazing at yearbooks and current refrigerator-door-loiterers across Spokane County—will have the chance to see these tweens' "lovely smiles."

"No thanks," my daughter tells the photographer, posing for her picture fully masked, eyes showing fierce and glinting above her black fabric mask. "I'd like an accurate representation of this reality," she says. Later, she tells me, she thought to herself: "I dissent."

She also says she felt like she was in a dystopian novel, and it was her job, as protagonist, to change things.

The following week, she starts a blog about her experiences, called *The President of Everything Goes to School*, to document this version of the world—one in which students complete a nightly health attestation regarding their symptoms, engage in contact tracing, wear masks and remain six feet apart at all times, carry all their belongings rather than using lockers (too close together), and submit all assignments virtually, to reduce exposure. Writes my eleven-year-old:

> During the school day we're on our computers way too much in my opinion, but then again, technological evolution in the classrooms is about as real as the fact that Eleanor Roosevelt was First Lady of the United States. Today, it was after school that I had tea and cookies, and I filled my tea with way too much honey, as usual. You know how sugar works in the human body? That's kind of how my morale goes at school.

I laugh, and share her post with friends, but I'm also concerned. Will the world still be there by the time she's of voting age? What about the eagles? And how can we prepare for this winter? At our place, we're building a tree house and planning an at-home carnival. We'll walk the river valley dressed as dragons and unicorns, and we'll talk about xenophobia and sexism and racism as realities, as well as what land conservation and ownership means. And my daughter will call me out on areas in which I need to grow, quote her favorite congresswoman, Alexandria Ocasio-Cortez, for whom my daughter has made a comic strip, with AOC in a superhero outfit.

RAISED BY FERNS

When I was a girl, fairy-sized people wandered the temperate rainforests of the coastal Northwest. I knew in my spore of spores that when I stayed motionless beneath trees, the tiny people were nearby, under the vanilla leaf and arching cedars with their lace curtains hanging low. If I saw a deer fern flick its dew or a sorrel rustle its shamrock face, those were the little people running home.

This is what my brother told me when I was four or five, and I believed him. He was an authority because he protected me from mean boys and didn't hurt me yet.[1]

When the rain hit a leaf, or an insect or bird wagged a branch, I believed it really was a small human, and that if I sat still long enough, I'd see one. So I would go into the woods and find a cozy spot and be very, very still for hours, waiting. During these times I witnessed many birds making nests, insect paths through the bark floor, and the ways filtered light moves and offers itself to chlorophyll of woodland species stage by stage. I never saw a fairy-sized person, but I didn't stop believing. I think this must be

---

[1] It's hard to say what *yet* means here—we're not headed into a story of abuse, but it is key to note that at this point in my life, my brother had not yet run me over with his bicycle, tied me to a tree, nor burned a bug alive under a jar. Nor had he hung my dolls from their necks from the ceiling of my room, shot me with a BB gun, nor dated my best friend. None of these things will happen in this story. My brother, when I'm four—to the best of my memory—had been a protector. Once, he pulled me from the ocean. Once, he yelled at bullies. Later, he'll face some typical adjustments of a child in a loving but inconsistent home. Some of these adjustments will result in discord with his sister (me). All of them will result in long-term psychological effects.

what religion is—to be patient and attentive, earnest of intention, and able to so clearly imagine something, you don't need for it to prove itself to you. You still hope it will, and you live in that hope. And it smells delicious there: like bark-rot and new berry blossoms, petrichor and feather.

When I read Margaret Wise Brown's *Fur Family*, the tiny book with the shaggy cover, I thought it was written about those little people—the ones we all probably believed existed, before growing up erased our imaginations. The little people were just like the big people, except more afraid, and they scurried faster, because they had to. I felt like I had a whole family of selves inside me, some furred and some not furred and some scared and some most at home under a mushroom, or in the glade of ferns where I might have easily been a rabbit or another furred creature.

*

In Virginia Woolf's iconic *A Room of One's Own*, she writes, "It is much more important to be oneself than anything else. . . . Think of things in themselves."[2]

*

When people used to ask me about my formative religion, I would often say I was raised transcendentalist, though in further study I realize what we were doing was closer to pagan or mythos or anarchy.

When people ask me where I grew up, I name a watershed or two—maps make more sense when drawn at the boundaries of

---

2 Immanuel Kant, "thing-in-itself" (German: Ding an sich), and later, W. C. Williams, in *Paterson*, "Say it! No ideas but in things."

each geography's highest elevations, sloped down where the water goes—into valleys and streams and rivers—and when people ask me about my family, I jokingly say, "Oh, I was raised by ferns."[3]

It's a half-truth—I was raised, of course, by books, borrowed from libraries, and by barns, and rivers and floods—but it's also more than a half-truth; it's an unfurling frond—you can see in it the way something might spiral out, like a snail shell or a mathematical sequence or the small, palm-sized universe of falling in love. Something potent—from the Latin *potentia*, "power, might, or force"—green, or a nameless color, with its own potential. Regardless of what's around it, so long as there's shade.

*

When you lie in a glade of bracken fern, on your back, by day the light filters through so that beyond the lacy fronds it's primarily shadow and web—the spiders following filaments, the sun-gleam riding each thread as if the light's alive. And at night in that same bed of fronds you find the moon is a close lamp that glimmers a blue-gray song, like a whale eye, knowing, or wondering, wandering as you do from your solitary spot among what you feel is the best family in the world—shades of green and gray and yellow-brown, "plotted and pieced"/ "fickle, freckled"—sori on the undersides of fern-blades saying hello with their congregations of spores all gathered in earthy praise.

---

[3] When I say I was raised by ferns, I don't mean I was actually raised by ferns—to believe that magic would be ridiculous; it would mean I am not of this world. When I say I was raised by ferns, I mean what my husband means when he says:

Maya, you aren't the demographic for anything,

when I apologize for not understanding culture, religion, or dominant capitalist traditions and as an excuse, mutter, *Don't mind me, I was raised by ferns.*

"Those who have paid any attention to colours, must be aware that it is very difficult to give colours for every object that appears in nature; the tints are so various, and the shades so gradual, they would extend to many thousands: it would be impossible to give such a number," writes P. Syme in *Werner's Nomenclature of Colours*. It's true. What color is the bracken fern? There isn't an accurate square to describe it here, but it's closest to siskin green, and the sword fern closer to sap green or pistachio green, or, in animal, the underside of lower wings of orange tip butterfly or neck of eider drake.

Here where the earth is the underside of a lepidoptera or neck of a bird, damp and bumpy through your clothes, smelling of roots and the decay of last year's plants, you feel at home. You're with your plant group—the one that follows you around the human-named geographies, its rhizomatic[4] roots below you joining and stemming and joining again, a whole network of water and mineral and salt anchoring the plant, and you, to the soil.

*

When we moved—which was frequently—we were allowed to pack and bring one fruit-sized-box of our things, the boxes durable/reusable ones, like those apple crates with the tops that nest over the bottoms like a shell in a shell. This culling of personal

---

[4] I have always known what a rhizome was, but I learned the literary theory only last year.

My first reaction was: rhizome isn't a theory, it's a *verb*. It's a way of being. It's the deep underground of the fern world. It's not something for you to appropriate into another critical metaphor in order to understand literature you don't write.

I admit this was a bit harsh. I mean, my life was rhizome theory. I didn't understand how folks got so into family trees, the lineage branching back to some sole source, a familial closeness, permanence. What was permanence?

property was a practical way to determine what came along—it needed to fit in the car or van or whatever vehicle we all went into when we left our latest rental—and meant we could keep any relics we found precious, so long as they were small. (This did on occasion elicit from me a tantrum, as when a friend's father built for me, on my seventh birthday, a large plywood, hand-painted bean-bag toss, and my mother, so that I would not cry upon our relocation, secretly gave it away to the local school and told me "They stole it, honey"—so that I would be furious at someone else instead of her. Of course I realized the reason we'd left it behind was that it wouldn't fit in the car, but I was furious anyway, as it was mine, and mine, and mine, and the largest and likely most painstakingly made thing I'd ever possessed. Later that winter, my father gave me a crisp five-dollar bill—the largest I'd ever held—to purchase a worn wooden jewelry box at a flea market, and I have that possession to this day.) In my "taking along" box, besides a few shells and rocks and a vial of apple stems I kept for superstition, I made a whole world of tiny, tiny animals and a few small teddy bears—about an inch tall, like you see on key chains in variety stores or gumball machines—and I made them little fabric coats from my sewing scraps, and little billiard cloth hats, and paper sets against which we'd perform plays, which I scripted and cast with the little animal characters. I stored my collection in an old Sarah Jo's Caramels box—about 3 x 6 x 8 inches—with a lid that opened and tucked in at the edge so the contents would not spill if jostled. And this box fit inside the larger apple box, so I still have it, now, and my children love to see what "funny junk" I kept, the kinds of things that children obtain for free or for one penny at a thrift store, which to me were the transportable treasures of a shifting, unpredictable world.

*

The first time I read a poet who I felt understood me (Whitman came close with his blades of grass, but there was something still too mannish about him, or too adult, or too American), I was standing in the Village Books' basement stacks in Bellingham, Washington, near the narrow but well-informed poetry section, which at the time was just out from the east brick wall. The store hadn't yet been remodeled, so it still held the mortar dust of the late 1990s, which is the decade when I was an undergraduate English major at Western. I knew almost nothing about contemporary poetry—I'd read mostly pre-1950s works that we all encountered in high school then—and except for one poetry course, which I took as an elective, had never formally studied the subject. But I knew my teacher had brought several visiting poets later that year, and I pulled out the slender volume left after a reading I didn't make it to—I had to work—*Cathedral of the North* by Connie Voisine.

Besides "Cameo," a poem that made my esophagus ache, a poem on what it felt like to come of age an immigrant and impoverished in rural Maine, hoarding coins in a sock to pay for the fancy privilege of an automatic car wash; or the line later, in "Rosary," "There is a weed we can eat"; the third poem that I felt undressed me, laid me naked there in that basement room, was "What Was So Beautiful About the Father," a seven-page piece that wove lineated verse and prose sections, what was then being casually dubbed "the hybrid lyric." Besides this new-to-me form, what delighted me most was specifically the moment when Voisine explicates the viscerality of understanding one's own complicity in a system, in a metaphor that is larger than a family, an image that contains lineage and mythos and history and, "in [her] small scrap of world, [her] father is / fragile

[...] and cannot withstand / fate and evil, equivalents." In this poem, her father was a logger, and his physical body was injured; whereas my father drove a tow truck, sold goods from Mexico in flea markets, and was psychologically damaged from his mother's death—they were not the same—and yet, I saw there myself, one of the ways I felt about my life, spoken so plainly and clearly I thought it should have been its own theory in a thick, expensive textbook:

> Being poor is my father.
> A Russian doll series, the largest
> is this Evil, and it encloses the doll of Poor.
> My father is the next doll, he
> disappears into Poor while completely containing
> me. I am lucky, the smallest doll
> whose features are plain, barely articulated
> by the brush, the one whose body won't
> open. Who can't bear that she is the reason
> the others' sturdy, wood torsos have split.

I had never heard a clearer explanation for my childhood—and now adult—psychology than this. Not in my education courses, where I knew I was supposed to believe myself the typical "middle child" in a house of "addiction," not in other cultural examinations of rural poverty (though I recognized many of my classmates and people in my towns), not in the workbooks my high school guidance counselor thrust upon me after my best friend died in a car crash when I was fifteen and supposed to be "finding my identity" through exercises. They all felt like the wrong clothes, the wrong realities. Here, in this very basic immigrant story, was a jewel in the middle of coal, "barely articulated / by the brush, the one whose body won't / open."

*

Whenever we moved, I said goodbye to my present glade and wood and in the new wild places found a forest or field, shadows flicking across. In each place, I didn't grow too close to other children—what was the point? They were often cruel and banal and I found thinking this way made it easier to leave. But I did get to know the plants, and by knowing them, could find them again. Leaving one habitat for another in the same kind of ecosystem—poverty towns—I found my fern friends: "Hello, sword, licorice, maidenhair, deer, and wood"—I'd say to each, upon arrival. "I see you've come along too!" Some children learn to count on specific recurring chain restaurants or fast-food joints, or holidays with grandparents and other extended relatives. I learned to trust the fronds.[5]

*

We know Margaret Wise Brown from *Goodnight Moon* or *The Runaway Bunny*, or maybe *The Diggers*—in these, she's weird,

---

[5] An index of ferns in my memoir manuscript:

"Library/Van": "the tangle of maple and alder, sword fern and salmonberry, through the field of hay grass and thistle with the nettled edge."

"Complete the Sentence": "Or maybe her cold outdoor pots have been full of ferns she needs to move indoors."

"Maslow's Hierarchy": "If they walked the roads alone—long, dark, full of ferns—"

"Landscape Anxiety"—"Where I was, it was green—ferns, moss, ferns and moss on trees. Too thick to see too far. You had to get to the beach or the field if you wanted a view. But the forest and moss was safe. And the creeks chunky and full of rocks." And "the mountains and ferns so far away." And "I say, it's tearing me open into something un-fern-like. It's un-mossing me."

And for *bracken:*

"I spend large chunks of summer in a hammock under a tree, watching the leaves. The bees. We planted brackens there years ago, and they frond up, knowing."

but my favorite is that fur family. The characters are bear-like and "smaller than most," and "lived in a warm wooden tree." The father puts on his coat in the mornings and goes "away out into his little fur world" (just like my father), the mother bathes the child in a basin of water heated on the stove (just like my family), and the child embarks "to play in the wild wood where they lived," a "wild wild wood," she emphasizes, where the little fur child learns everything by experience and observation—pulling a fish from the river and then letting it go, catching a bug ("The bug didn't have any fur. It was shiny and had little wings"), and then letting it go—and then finally catching—and, yes, letting go—"a little tiny tiny fur animal," which looks exactly like him—making us wonder if the whole world is a miniature version inside of another world just like it, all nested in sequence down to the ones that we can't articulate with our brushes.

The fur child plays alone all day in the forest and at the end of the day the sky is "wild and red" and he must run for home, which makes us see this book's kingdom is both magical and frightening, like a real world, like the one we are in outside the book, that the home inside the tree inside the book inside the doll inside the self is just an articulation of what we are learning and storing and sorting and escaping and trying again tomorrow.

*

The ferns you typically see depicted in children's books are bracken, sword, and wood.

In Coraline Bickford-Smith's *Fox and Star*, Fox curls up to sleep safely in the wood ferns. The book never says the word *fern*, but the drawing shows them with their longer, lower pinnae, the triangle of asymmetrical lace fanning up.

"There is a woman's veil shrunk to a religion of brown," ends Melissa Kwasny's poem, "Fern." Of course, she means the fronds have gone dark, the rhizome dormant.

And in Inger Christensen's *alphabet,* a book-length ode to natural history, organized both as abecedarian and by the mathematical pattern of Fibonacci's sequence, she says secondly, after apricot trees(!), as the numbers' first sum of itself, that "bracken exists," and so the world is born and borne through the bracken—

*

In *The Velveteen Rabbit,* it is the bracken fern where the boy "always made the Rabbit a little nest," and it was in this place the rabbit always watched the sun cross the sky and the ants scurry and at night the white moths come out, and from his gentle place beneath these ferns he saw his own kind:

> One evening, while the Rabbit was lying there alone, watching the ants that ran to and fro between his velvet paws in the grass, he saw two strange beings creep out of the tall bracken near him.

Indeed when the Velveteen Rabbit recognized other creatures like himself, he was in the ferns, and so it was with child-Maya. The long green arcs of light and shadow, spore-jeweled, in moist areas. I could count on them. A dormant fern is still there; its roots say so. They rhizome and grow, and they send into themselves new selves, up-springing and unfurling. Spore, spiral, and grow. Repeat.

*

That story by Steven Millhauser, "In the Reign of Harad IV," the "maker of miniatures" who lives at court creates smaller and smaller worlds nested inside one another, and "It was said that no matter how closely you examined one of the Master's little pieces you always discovered some further wonder." This is not unlike the nested curiosities in one's own mind, except when you look up and out and then look back, you must work a long, long time to get close enough to see the smallest details, and sometimes I wonder: if you spend too long away from those miniature worlds, might you lose the ability to recognize them altogether?

And what does it feel like, anyway, to be so certain that the smaller nested worlds of yourself would be articulated by anyone else, and that those little selves wouldn't be made to feel ashamed by the makers for taking up space?[6]

*

---

6 Spore Couture

Maidenhair fit my measurements from 1979 to 2005, but then I was inland, away, the bright lace and black stem absent from my days.

Licorice fern is adaptable and great for layering—whether in the temperate rainforests of the Olympic Peninsula or the dark parts of ravine-forests in central Oregon—where it finds the rare trees that sport mosses.

Swords make an excellent skirt and even better floor—their material durable and though youth sometimes harvest them for city folks who want "a natural look" in their greenhouse vases, they belong in the wild, the coast, the Inland Northwest, all over, their undersides thick with healing spores. The way I tell it to my children is this: "One nice thing about plants is that there isn't a bully among them, but if accidentally the nettle stings you and your skin becomes a rash of small, burning volcanos simmering in their strangeness, the dark sword growing nearby will provide you an antidote on its under-spores." Nature's antidote: medicine for what stings nearby. This is how nature does it—you can almost always find a cure for what harms you growing right next door.

A friend says that my "work" house in Ellensburg—in which I live part time because I must commute and have a second place to lie my head—is like the little house that I kept inside myself[7] for so long, even when I lived in other houses.[8] We reason perhaps it has always existed inside me, and when I purchase it, I am really just moving into what's been there all along. It's the birds, she says, and the box and star. And the bugs, I want to say. But I know no one's very into beetles.

In my little house I read more. I wake up and make coffee and I read until I run. Then, in the evening, I make tea and read until I sleep. I don't have internet, and I prefer it that way. Sometimes when I am here I pretend I am old, or Annie Dillard. "How we spend our days is of course how we spend our lives." I think about how quiet it is and I hum a little trying to get the feel of it. I watch the fire.

---

7 By the time I was grown I realized everybody has a house inside, and in my inside, there is more than one house. Inside the house is a Book and inside the book is this Forest and in the forest is the Ferns who raised me and in the ferns is a Bunny, a Girl, Another Book . . . each section is a nesting house inside the other. Each is a song inside a song inside a self, is a poem-spell.

8 House Rules:

Hold your spores close and keep them in their sori until dry season. Then you can let them go—but hope they land on moist ground.

If you're wilting, lean on other ferns.

You can thrive between rocks if you find a spot of decay plus water. You can turn almost anything into food.

Some ferns are dimorphic (they grow both fertile and infertile fronds, like deer fern), and some have both fertile and infertile pinnae on the same leaf (like the evergreen sword fern). All are still ferns.

Some ferns are evergreen, some deciduous, some semi-deciduous. All are still ferns.

The fire is an easy one. I miss chopping wood, but I do like to flick the switch and watch the flames leap into the false logs. And I like the glow of the false coals. It's cozy, even though I know it's not real wood, real coals. It's one way I'm willing to pretend.

The fire is real, though, even if it is just hot burning gas. It has enough realness to it that I can look into it and pretend there is a cave there, or a glen, where I might create worlds.

*

I read the *Velveteen Rabbit* by the light of the moon, full this month on a Thursday: "It was light now, for the moon had risen. All the forest was beautiful, and the fronds of the bracken shone like frosted silver. In the open glade between the tree-trunks the wild rabbits danced with their shadows on the velvet grass."

The velvet grass, where I found my first teacup, cracked and rosetted. By the shores of an ocean. Inland, where I still lie down on my back in the bracken, writing my charms. Where still I try to witness the world moving by being quite calm. A house, another house, a forest.

*

Sometimes in spring I go out under the maple and watch the vertical stems in dormant state to see if they are doing. By this I mean I want to catch them in the act of sending out their fiddleheads—their fairy people. I never do—it seems to happen only when the world is sleeping, or working, or catching up on being human. The ferns are very private about it. The next time I look, there are small, coiled shapes tight against the root of hair-mess from last year, bright and green, as much a people as I am a people, ready to expand into galaxies.

EPILOGUE:
THE PRIVILEGE (UN)BUTTON

BLUE TONGUE

The river was full of dead deer the October my husband first ended his affair.

Mysterious corpses, bloated like driftwood, our nostrils sensing them before we saw them, accrued on banks and gravel bars. We could not help but imagine each limping to the shores to drink, then lying down and dying and rotting there as if it was the river that killed them. At each new doe, I wondered if we should exit and portage back across fields and rocks. If we kept on, would we soon be dead as well?

I had never seen anything like this, never felt such doom gather in my chest. (Had I?) I wanted to live for a minute in the relief I'd felt when my husband stopped seeing Julie, but my body heard what the earth said: The crisis is just beginning. I sensed it, up out of what I jokingly call my embodied consciousness, the powers I'd accumulated during my own transformations. I felt them rising, rhizomatic, in my own animal limbs. Does it sound dramatic? It felt dramatic.

*

Our family often kayaked this stretch of river where it winds through the valley southwest of the dam, still meandering slow and full of crawdads and trout and overhung with willows, alder, downed wood casting shadowy snags where you can catch things if you're looking to catch things, before speeding up just a little toward the end, making its baby ripples, the kind no one gets hurt in, but the rocks grow a little larger, toddler-sized rocks, a place only dangerous if you look away too long from the danger, this easy sand-ridge where people teach their kids to fly-fish.

Our children don't fly-fish, but they do float the river, hanging off the edges of our kayaks, stopping to jump from each gravel bar's thigh-deep water into the drop-offs, drinking fizzy waters and eating snacks. Chilled-out kids, stress-free kids. What I want for them. What I thought *we* wanted for them. What we might want together, still, I hoped, even if my husband was having doubts about everything else. We could work through it, I reasoned. I had a lot of practice in overcoming shit, I reminded him. This was a thing we could figure out together.

On the river, though, something was wrong—the air full of death. We all braced for it. We'd seen dead beavers, inhaled them, the bile making us retch, but this was no beaver—it turned out to be deer, multiple deer carcasses, oddly placed like objects on a horror film set. Inexplicable, new stench every few hundred feet. The first was beached on a rock bar in the middle of the river, no wounds, just bloat. A dead deer like a dead seal, hauled in from a nightmare.

Wanting to believe the occurrence singular, we played a guessing game, used our imaginations.

"Maybe it was hit by a car on the bridge and fell into the water," said our daughter.

"Maybe a poacher had to pitch it in to hide the evidence," I said.

"I think they are zombies," said our son.

Our son—just nine—rode in my kayak, and our daughter with her dad, and the leaves blazed into yellows and the air mostly smelled like things going to sleep. The season was fall in every way: the last paddle, melancholy-beautiful; everything gilded / stained with the fact of my husband just cutting off his early-stage affair with a woman he met in climbing school. While I taught my summer overload classes, they had spent the months lying and sneaking around: bringing her to the family lake place (with our children, who mentioned it to me and were surprised I hadn't known), buying her gifts (I learned of from our credit card bill), later leaving the kids alone while he and his affair went kayaking or floating the river, or some other adventure date (not something we yet did together; how I had longed for this possibility in the almost-here years!), pretending like there was nothing unusual about it, repeatedly insisting I was imagining things.

No, of course I don't have feelings for her.
. . . Don't be ridiculous.
. . . No, I didn't buy her a birthday present?
. . . Oh, I was out with climbing friends . . .

Climbing friends? He'd never had climbing friends . . . how could I be anything but happy for him? How could I suspect anything cruel? He even told our friend Laura how cute it was that I seemed jealous! how delightful, how funny, how affirming for him. And to me: *Babe, don't be silly. It's really just a friendship.* Then later, *You don't want me to have friends. You're so controlling.*

I felt all the things anyone in my situation might feel. Of course I wanted him to have friends; I also wanted him to be honest. Have you been betrayed by your life partner? Of course I asked him—for the love of god, on anything sacred, on my C-section scars, on my impending breast lump ultrasound, on the years I'd given him more than one thousand percent when he was forced to resign from his coaching job, on whatever he might hold holy (Jesus? The children? His own dick?)—to please stop seeing her, or please stop lying, before it made things more difficult, no matter the direction it all went next. Before it harmed our children, irrevocably. I begged him to, at the very least, be direct with me. Hoping, as one does in my situation, that they weren't too far gone, believing him and not, my body bewildered with myself for doubting, and he finally, too reluctantly, agreed it wasn't "just a friendship."

That first time they ended it, he relayed to me that she told him, like an invitation, "If you were single, I'd love to date you."

She'd love to do something, even if he wasn't single. She was a risk-taker, an adventure-seeker, young and unattached and easy and free, and he finally admitted what she really wanted was an affair. So, for the first of many attempts at letting it go, he let it go—he said. And I believed him.

And I didn't believe him.

*

On the river, each next deer draped itself, camouflaged like a water-logged trunk, disguised, so without our olfactory senses, without having seen the first so clearly, we may not have noticed. If we just looked at the beauty around us, if we ignored the clarity of what one sense was telling us, we could almost believe there was nothing amiss.

*

What does the body know that we don't? Mine tried to tell me, but I wouldn't accept it—even with all my worst-case-preparing, my Cassandra-ing, my nights damp with fear—how would I know, how could I know, that in another year and a half, I'd be sitting across from my lawyer (*my* lawyer!), discussing custody and assets, how I might, by working more-more-more, be able to keep my children at least part time in our home—discussing all the ridiculous logistics of splitting a life already split in two for one of us, so the other could have more of the whole he'd already claimed.

How could I know, when they first "ended" their dalliance, that in a year and a half, every sleeping moment would be plagued by violent, clairvoyant nightmares? That waking hours would be dread and terror? How could I know that I would find myself begging my husband to let me and my children stay in our house, despite its inflated value I couldn't afford? That finally I'd tell my lawyer about the violence, my husband's drinking, the fear we all had; that my lawyer would explain gently that because I hadn't reported it, the courts would only see what was evident: a mother who—before COVID years—had left town for work every Tuesday through Thursday, sometimes Monday through Thursday; a father who drove his children to school, like a very good nanny, a father who—despite this midlife crisis, despite past actions that led to investigation, resignation from coaching—held no criminal record. A father whose family was law, whose family was church, whose brother had also cheated and had their parents' support, whose family believed only in the divine rights of sons, not the bodies or lives of women who bore their sons' seeds, whose family had money to hire an attorney, who would stop at nothing. And that—as my (ex) husband said over and over, his eyes steel blue not firmament blue not baby blue but metal and unflinching—"Washington is a no-fault state."

Which meant, I learned, by unlearning love, that the laws were written by men to protect men, and patriarchy said my body and mind and blood and babies belonged half to him, my house and car and insurance and labor belonged half to him, who after his initial attempt to stop, and his second attempt to hide it, and his third attempt to lie, and his fourth—however many times they said it was over—had later openly cheated and vacationed and taken "his half"; and none of that mattered, it's redundant to write it, a waste of my words; a waste of our minds; our whole HOA was half his, my retirement my babies my stardust my waking my sleeping my fitful not-sleeping hours, my life.

*

Bluetongue is a hemorrhagic disease, caused by a virus spread by biting flies. Fevered and dehydrated, sick deer find bodies of water to drink and die by the banks, or wading into the water to cool off, perish on islands or float downstream, their bodies bloating and stinking. When we called the Department of Fish and Wildlife after the river-adventure-turned-horror float, they said they could not remove them—they were part of the natural cycle of things. "But it looks like a terrible movie," I had said, grasping, when my husband relayed the message.

It felt both Real and Not Real, constructed to create an emotional response.

"And it seems like it would be dangerous for the other animals." But it wasn't dangerous, they said, and carnage notwithstanding, those corpses were going to rot there into the winter months.

We did not kayak the river again that fall; and by spring, with the deer gone, the memory of them over that stretch of river, and my husband starting Affair 2.0, their secret thrill-and-lust phase, I worried around every corner, wondering and waiting for the ghost of that fear. For Mother's Day, we had a tradition of starting our annual float, but residual memory stopped me. Was it the recall, anticipatory anxiety, those Cervidae mammals filling the waterways with their hooves angled strangely, their eyes rolled back or open or closed, that made me feel so weird embarking on this thing I normally loved? River things, outdoor things, all things—my muscle memory, struggling from years of gaslighting, from Long COVID, from the reality of a failing marriage in which I had done so much domestic management, all of childbirth and baby care, so much of the parenting and financial labor—felt my age: early forties, worried about the world, the earth's inhabitants, human, animal, and plant. I couldn't help but note some proximal off-ness: an echo in the pit of me, that foreboding, narrative dread I carried everywhere. Something was *wrong*. This was before the worst of it, when it could have gone the other way: a light affair, a return to trying, radical honesty, growth. I wanted growth, but I could feel the truth: the planet, my body, my family were all in danger. Like all of us. From without, obviously—but now, I slowly confessed to myself, from within. And, another feeling, creeping like a foreboding smell: wasn't it me? Wasn't this my doing? Hadn't I left my family, to work? Wasn't he lonely at night when I went to teach, or when, downstairs in the same house on my laptop, I plunked away at my second job, trying to secure permanence, privilege? Hadn't I encouraged him, when I saw him slipping in those years after losing his job, to sign up for adventure classes? Didn't I, after all, help him make space for this affair to happen?

*

Long-term effects of gaslighting include gaslighting oneself. Include panic attacks. Include anxiety, insomnia, dread. Include, in some cases, paranoia and self-blame. Everything is suspect, and everything seeds doubt. I didn't want to believe my sweet, former-youth-group-president husband, the man for whom and with whom I'd built this world for nearly a quarter century, would be the one to destroy it. I wanted to believe, against proof, in his goodness, in beauty. I wanted to believe he simply needed my help. And I wanted to help him. But eight months after he had "ended" their affair that fall of the dead deer float, months during which my suspicions flared, my guilt deepened over my own doubt, my mouth said things like *please be honest, I love you,* after his anger and denial and promises made me turn on myself, I learned what of course was always going to be true: they had been secretly seeing each other again. For months. Does the timeline of trying matter? He couldn't stop lying. I couldn't stop letting him.

*

During those months, I felt like I was always on the river, corpses ahead. I could see, but didn't trust, the splendor of my own life.

Alone with him at night in our bed, our children sleeping across the hall, their little bodies unaware, I begged my husband to just tell me the truth so we could make decisions, with all the information in front of us, together. I laid out my own vulnerabilities, again, explaining as best I could my own midlife anxieties, my flaws, the ways I felt we could grow together, expand, keep our children in their safe worlds. I begged him, please meet me there.

Desperate, I even wrote to his affair partner, appealing to her as a fellow woman. I told her my husband was responsible for his own actions, and she for hers, that I wasn't interested in vilifying her. Asked if she'd like to talk honestly about how we might all move forward. Desperately, as if our lives might matter to her. Desperately reminded her there were children involved.

*

When I was a kid, we used to have this Volkswagen Rabbit, forest green. On the freeway, my dad would pull up very close behind a semitruck, practically under it, so you couldn't even see the mudflaps girl bent backwards, her breasts up and her hair flown back. My dad would inch our car so tight to the truck it was as if an invisible thread hooked us together, then he'd put the Rabbit in neutral, and draft. I felt terrified we might get wedged underneath, or somehow crash into the ditch or median, be flung off the highway into the yellow Scotch broom in some horrible cosmic breaking of orbit. But when I spoke—my small voice floating from the back seat—he simply laughed and said, "Relax! We're getting a free ride!"

That calculated proximity, that intentional capitalization of physics and force pulled us, dangerously, at seventy miles an hour, not wasting any gasoline, my body's natural survival instincts ridiculous and unwelcome.

I have always been training my cells, my muscles, to live in a state of suspended disbelief, training into silence my body's fear response. Training myself not to listen to my brain, not to think like a child who feels something bad is going to happen, not to pay attention to my cells' deep knowing, not to count the ways, not to catalog the ways.

*

At his work office, his real estate appointments, in our car parked at local gardens where once we took family photos, the maples snowberry Oregon grape watching, at climbing events for Mountain School, via WhatsApp, in our home, in his brother's basement, in his dreams. In the river, on the bridges, in the restaurants, in the bars. In my kayaks, with my frisbees, with my bank account, in my body. On my trails. At our waterfall, on our ridge. In my subconscious. In his own.

*

But the body holds each fact. When you've been told one thing but something else is real, when the body moves that cognitive dissonance dissonance dissonance into its operative register, when you learn to live with the dread panic, to go on, dysregulated, you eventually go partially numb.

Numb, and still wondering what might be Real. Was I Real? Was my life? Had the deer in the river the year prior been a mirage, something I'd imagined or dreamed?

Had he even, ever, stopped seeing her, any of the half dozen times he said that he had?

The children hadn't yet learned to lie to themselves, to cope, so they noticed his behavioral changes more clearly, voiced them directly. They'd say, "He's mean to you." "He's always grumpy." "He likes her more than us." "We don't like her." "We don't trust him." I tried to do what I thought was best—tell them "it must be hard to feel that way, your father loves you, he's going through a tough time, he's trying his best," even, because he said so over and over, I repeated it: She's just a friend, and other things I wanted to believe. As I learned to listen to myself again, to trust what my body felt, their bodies felt, what was real, I stopped defending him. Together, the children and I dreaded his mood swings. We dreaded his car. We knew she was in our home with him when we weren't here: Menstrual evidence in the bathroom. A feeling of them in the air. Neighbors texting me that her car had been in the driveway, then inside the garage. Sometimes I slipped back into pretending things were going to be okay—to protect my children, I think, maybe out of fear of what else my now-ex, still husband, might do. I protected him when he was my husband, then my kind-of-separated-still-madly-sleeping-together-figuring-it-out husband, then my ex but not-yet ex-husband—because I was afraid.

Look, I have been a woman all my life. I was terrified he could enact the punishments he threatened. I was afraid of how else he might hurt us, what else he could do.

"If you tell her," he would say, his eyes knives, "this is over." He meant, as he held me, crying, then comforted me, spent the night wrapped around me, that if I told his now-openly-acknowledged affair partner the truth about his back-and forth, his uncertainty, his time in bed with me, that he would take my children, prove once and for all to everyone that I was, as he put it, crazy. That old trick: from a place of trust and power, simply manipulate someone into submission. Then, when they feel defeated, tell them they're broken. With distance, it's obvious. And even now—from his status as ex and my status as primary parent—he texts me: "If you were a healthy mother." "You need help." "You clearly can't do this."

*

The deer around our home sport lumps on their joints and near their hooves, and sometimes limp, and I've wondered if they have some kind of viral disease that causes deformity. The four of us have lived in our house, near the Little Spokane, with deer and coyotes and moose and herons and racoons and bald eagles, for a decade. Our relationship to the land and its inhabitants in this river valley brought us into conservation efforts, community. And over the years, we've seen, together, climate change firsthand: fewer river otters, fewer beavers, less frequent moose sightings, warmer water. I worry about the trout and I worry about the deer and I worry about everybody. The type of biting fly that infect deer with bluetongue have midges that like shallow and lukewarm places and thrive near muddy banks. Standing pools of spring runoff and stagnant back eddies create ideal conditions for these insects to breed, and deer that survive the hemorrhagic illnesses can develop lumps and limps. Our deer might be coincidentally injured, but I cannot help yoking them together. (I will learn later the population faces a new calamity: chronic wasting disease. This, too, is fatal, and I can't help them.)

*

When my son was born late, blue, maternal instinct told me to protect him. I was, at the time, a non-tenure-track lecturer at a Jesuit university that advertised itself as "fighting for social justice" but did not in 2012 offer maternity benefits, so I had waited until signing my annual contract before filing for twelve weeks of unpaid FMLA leave. From extra teaching gigs, I'd saved enough to have a few months' break from school, to take care of my babies—my first time not working outside the home since I'd turned fifteen. I spent those weeks nursing my son, applying therapeutic massage and other techniques to help him catch up to the expected benchmarks for fine and gross motor skills, wrapping him in a cocoon of care and immune support. His sister, just three, learning to read. Learning things sometimes go wrong. Learning how to move through it. Together, she and I took care of her brother, while her father traveled with his athletes to California and Texas and across our state. By the time my son turned six months old, he began hitting his developmental milestones "on time," and I returned to the job we desperately needed me to be working, which, even at its below-poverty wages, still brought in more than my husband's assistant distance coach salary.

Within that year, my husband faced an investigation that ended in his resignation. He spent two weeks curled in a ball on our couch. I took on adjunct work at two more colleges. I parented our two toddlers. Then I lucked into a more stable, better paying, tenure-track position. But in another town. My husband, recovering from his crisis, enrolling in real estate courses, asked that I commute, try it out short term, so he could start a new career, one that would—he promised—eventually become our main financial support. Why did I allow this path? Our home felt like something worth protecting. I thought I could probably manage for a while, until he found something more secure, or until we relocated our family. I don't know how "short term" turned into those first four years. I was, simply, barely surviving.

And then COVID hit. My son, with his less robust immune system, had it first, and then my husband and daughter, and finally me—from so much exposure, taking care of everyone like some kind of freaking martyr, that first spring before testing or vaccines were available, and I ended up with Long COVID. So did my son.

Medically vulnerable, emotionally exhausted, spiritually drained, I dreamed of nothing but rest. It must be near, I thought. Sabbatical, maybe, or the end of the pandemic, or maybe when my children were just old enough that they didn't need constant care. The future would be calmer, easier. I told myself that if I kept my head down and kept pulling, we'd get there. And my husband?—flailing, resting, recovering, starting his career in real estate, doing HOA work, skiing, playing, taking classes, taking on new hobbies, mountaineering. Eventually, I would be able to join him.

*

Naively, I thought for so long that what we both wanted for this family was a slow float on a healthy river. I thought we were both horrified by terror deer and other effects of climate change and human avarice, that we wanted to help our children grow honestly into who they are, to form internal compasses, to model that. And that someday, I might be able to rest.

*

When the deer reach the river, they drink but their thirst is not quenched. They collapse, weak and hallucinating. Their muscles and organs hemorrhage. Their heads swell, and their necks, their lips, their tongues. Within forty-eight hours, they will die, of dehydration or delirious drowning. Their lives undo quickly, from vital and lively to bloated, littered on riverbanks and gravel bars. Pocking the landscape with warnings, air spoiled with the stench of loss.

*

I know privilege is fragile. Especially when you claw your way into it from a tenuous place. Especially when the world is ending around you, when extreme weather events and mass viral outbreaks and endemic violence have made clear to everyone what so many of us knew already: America isn't the last safe place. There is no safe place. Our bodies, our children, the animals can tell.

But I wanted to make a home. A place from which these children could float or swim—and return—a place without constant dread. I once jokingly called my automatic garage door opener a "privilege button," wrote an essay around HOA rules. I tried, when I started this essay, to write in response to that—ACEs (Adverse Childhood Experiences) Scores, custody law, rental agreements. But I'm not simply navigating housing privilege versus rental privilege. I'm navigating something psychologically unmooring—something complex and monstrous and technical and ineffable. Something destabilizing on myriad levels, because I don't and can't trust anymore that my children's father will ever feel safe, or like home, for them again.

*

Sometimes it seems like we've been on that river for the last two and a half years. The deer are sometimes close together, with no breaks between, and other times, we float along for a few hundred feet, letting ourselves watch the kingfishers and plovers, the turtles sunning themselves, thinking maybe we'll see a moose crashing in the brush. We may have to paddle to stay out of the snags by shore, to keep our heads out of the overhangs, to avoid a rock. We don't mind paying attention, even getting cold or bitten by mosquitos. But we know around the next bend there is probably another familiar horror, and soon we think we can smell it, we can almost taste it, the matted fur and the suggestion of maggots and the eyes that can't see but still bulge with the idea of seeing.

Sometimes I feel like this trip on the beautiful river of corpses will never end, even though as I write this, my divorce is being finalized. There is still so much to navigate: selling our home, my children forced to live 40 percent of the time with the two people who want that, who want the money "owed" them, in our "no-fault" state, where a person can cheat and lie and harm his children, and his wife of nearly twenty-five years, and then take half of all assets, legally.

I think about those small fly midges who were just following some biological command to receive pleasure in a bite of blood.

The parallel is false and incomplete, but it makes more sense than my life. And it is happening at the same time. And it is dangerous to a creature. And that is worth noticing.

So is my body: what is she telling me? How can I relearn to listen, like my children do, to the instincts that exist to keep us safe? How can I live in dissonance and danger? How can I help my children trust themselves, develop ways to cope and self-regulate in a world that isn't getting better?

*

I still hold privileges. I have the financial resources to rent an apartment or duplex for my children and me, where we are required by law to still live, close to their father, within the district where they attend school. I have a tenured job, and a second job, which will mean future financial stability, even if (for the time being—until my son graduates, or I change careers) I must commute two days a week, three hours each way, to and from the primary one, spend extra hours online for the second. I have an able body, mental acuity, the power of language. Most importantly, I have my children 60 percent of the time. It isn't enough. But it must be enough.

I'm forty-four. I've worked hard, made sacrifices, blah blah. I followed those stupid-ass vows, gave up my health for others' dreams, blah blah blah. Now I'm losing my home. My children are losing their home. Their illusion of safety.

It's winter now, two years and several months after the river first swelled with dead deer, and our neighborhood in the HOA in

Spokane—where I thought we'd grow old, welcome our teens home from college, host holidays, rest in a hammock under the trees, where I'd write my next books—is covered in snow, strung with Christmas lights, their indigo glow. Inside my house, I begin to box up our things, thinking about what's around the next corner. Hope it's less chaotic. Hope I can predict, prepare. Know I cannot control. I list to myself, like prayer, my find-the-silver-lining criteria for a new place to live: on the bus route to my children's schools. Some natural light. A tree or two (or more!). Safety from sexual predators, driving distance to a trail, and the ability to venture, in my working car, to the woods and river, which hopefully will not be littered with deer carcasses, or across the wide state to the west side where I can occasionally see the ocean, which I hope will have sea stars, water the right temperature for seals to survive, and whales. Maybe whales! And if we can find it, it would be nice to have a garage to park the car in the winter, when the snow falls and the ice and slush deepen the sides of the streets, and things go dormant, and the fly midges die off, and the world resets, readies for another season, a world in which we might be able to go outside before it gets too hot and the forests burn. It would be nice if there were space in the garage for one kayak, three bicycles. And sure, it would be convenient if the garage had an automatic button—but I don't need it. I never did.

ACKNOWLEDGMENTS

Thank you to dear friends who were early and incisive readers (and listeners) of individual essays and ideas for essays, including Dawn Pichon Barron, CMarie Fuhrman, Ellie Kozlowski, Jennifer Marion, Rachel Mehl, Kathryn Nuernberger, Kate Reed, Liz Rognes, Marianne Salina, Alexandra Teague, Katie (Bellingham) Wisenor.

Thank you to those stalwarts who read the whole damn thing (some of you, multiple times!): Kate Lebo, Matt Martinson, Laura Read, Sharma Shields, Julie Stevenson—I'm honored you believed all along that *Ferns* would be a book.

Thank you to those whose support of my prose helped usher *Ferns* into being: Jim Churchill-Dicks, Tara Conklin, Sayantani Dasgupta, Carol Guess, Jonathan Johnson, Margot Kahn, Leyna Krow, Sam Ligon, Suzanne Paola, Kristen Millares Young, Kim Mitchell, Christine Nicolai, Gary Scott, Katie Scott, Sharma Shields, Ana Maria Spagna, Kami Westhoff, Elissa Washuta, Joe Wilkins.

To my Inland Northwest Jellyfish loves: may you feel the gratitude in our collective sting. Laura Read, Kathryn Smith, and Ellen Welcker, always.

Thank you to present and past students for inspiration and comraderies, most especially Leslee Caul, Brittany Helmick (LaPointe),

Jenn Lynn, J. Kropla, Brittany McCarrick, Foster McKinnell, Weston Morrow, Erica Reid, Janelle Serio, Gabby Triana. Water remembers us.

A special note of gratitude for my sister, RaineMarie Rose Miller (now Raine Proctor), who lived so much of this with me—field and river, flood and van life, *I got me a car it's as big as a whale*—and who read the essays as they were written. Thanks for suffering so many miles with my ongoing ramblings.

Thank you to my mother, Cindy Kelso, and my children, Zoey and Canyon.

Thank you to the generous writers who offered words of praise for this book: Jamie Ford, Kathryn Nuernberger, Sharma Shields, and Jess Walter.

Thank you, Jeremy Pataky. Porphyry Press feels, in many ways, like a kind of coming home.

I am grateful to editors of the following publications, for giving these essays their first places to live, especially Suzanne, Lisa, Ander, Jane, Jenny, Carla, Margot, Erin, and Polly. Polly, thanks for believing in my essay enough to nominate it for the Best American Series. The journals in which these essays first appear include:

> *Bellingham Review*: "He Worked as an Electrician. He Enjoyed Television. (His Obituary Was Plain.)"

Cincinnati Review: "Ruin Porn"

DIAGRAM: "Poverty Fires" (This essay also appears in the Bloomsbury textbook, *Environmental and Nature Writing*, 2nd edition.)

Guesthouse: "Sestina for Foragers"

Pleiades: "Letters to Francesca Woodman from Spokane and Farther West" (This also appeared as a reprint in Sage Hill Press's *Railtown Almanac*.)

River Styx: "Landscape Anxiety"

The Rumpus: "Complete the Sentence"

This Is the Place: Women Writing about Home (Seal Press, 2017): "The Privilege Button" (A selection/re-write of this was also reprised on the Humanities Washington blog and *Spark Magazine*.)

What She Might Think (blog of author Erin Pringle): "Library/Van" (as guest blogger)

Willow Springs: "Scavenger Panorama" (This was selected by Vivian Gornick as a Notable for *Best American Essays*, 2023.)

I also owe tremendous debts of gratitude to the following organizations for time, funding, or other resources that helped support this memoir: Centrum Port Townsend for a writing residency, St. Edmund (Teddy) Hall and Erica McAlpine at University of Oxford for a fellowship, Central Washington University for a sabbatical leave, Washington State Artist Trust for a fellowship.

Thank you to the Timberland Regional Library System, to Bob and (the late) Thea Pyle for letting me believe you needed help watering the garden, and for listening to my poems and teaching me about ferns; to Sarah Jo, Tom, and (the late) Nancy Parson for the hot baths, caramel edges, and rope swing over the ocean. Thank you to Uncle Fred and my father, Barry Miller, for teaching me to scavenge. Thank you, ongoingly, to the following rivers, tributaries, and watersheds for their gravity and levity: the Grays River, Little Spokane and Waikiki Springs, Whatcom Creek, Arch Cape Creek, Lower Columbia Watershed, and the Spokane Aquifer. Thank you to the thousands of ferns that held and hold me.

NOTES

This book would not exist without my tangle of ancestry and community. I want to especially thank the writers and their works cited in these essays, including those I admire as gospel and groundwater, and those who trouble me, in the order in which each source appears:

The Privilege Button
 Federico García Lorca, "Theory and Play of the Duende"; Wallace Stevens, "The Snowman"; E.D. Hirsch, *Dictionary of Cultural Literacy*; Barbara Ehrenreich, *Nickel and Dimed*

Scavenger Panorama
 Charlotte Bronte, *Jane Eyre*; Maria Semple, *Where'd you Go, Bernadette?*; Dr. Seuss, *The Cat in the Hat Comes Back*; The Talking Heads, "Once in a Lifetime"; Kenneth Grahame, *The Wind in the Willows*; Henry David Thoreau, "Walking"; Toni Morrison, "The Site of Memory"

Sestina for Foragers
 Francis Mayes, *The Discovery of Poetry*; Kate Lebo, *The Book of Difficult Fruit*; Barbara Ehrenreich, *Nickel and Dimed*

Poverty Fires
 Nietzsche, *Philosophy in the Tragic Age of the Greeks*; Rick

Barot, "The Garden"; William Faulkner, "Barn Burning"; Ray Bradbury, *Fahrenheit 451*; Henry David Thoreau, *Walden*

Complete the Sentence
Sabrina Orah Mark, "Everything Was Beautiful and Nothing Hurt"; Federico García Lorca, "Theory and Play of the Duende"

Maslow's Hierarchy of Needs
Abraham Maslow, "A Theory of Human Motivation"; Art Alexakis/Everclear, "I Will Buy You a New Life"; The Counting Crows, "Round Here"

Everything I Know about "Ordinary and Typical Human Beings Who Made it Into Heaven" I Learned from the Movie *Saint Ralph*
Brigit Pegeen Kelly, "Imagining Their Own Hymns" (used with permission of the publisher, Yale University Press)

Balsamroot's Arrow-Shaped Leaves Point in So Many Directions at Once
Robert Martone, "Scientists Discover Children's Cells Living in Mothers' Brains"

Letters to Francesca Woodman from Spokane and Farther West
Corey Keller and Julia Bryan, *Francesca Woodman*; Dr. Seuss, *The Foot Book: Dr. Seuss's Wacky Book of Opposites*

Landscape Anxiety
John Gardner, "The Art of Fiction: Notes on Craft for Young Writers"; Melissa Kwasny, "Tobacco"; Brigit Pegeen Kelly, email exchange; Byrd Baylor, *Everybody Needs a Rock*; *The Desert Is*

Theirs; *I'm in Charge of Celebrations*; Leo Leone, *Frederick*; Kaveh Akbar; Richard Hugo, *The Triggering Town*; Homer's *Odyssey*; Jon Krakauer, *Into the Wild*

Ruin Porn
Zoolander; Nathaniel Hawthorne, *The Scarlet Letter*; The Police, "Don't Stand So Close To Me"

The Metamorphosis
Rosalie Moffett, "The Nervous System;" Franz Kafka, "The Metamorphosis"; Dr. Seuss, *Yertle the Turtle*; H.D., *Notes on Thought and Vision* and *End to Torment: a Memoir of Ezra Pound*; Anne Carson, *Autobiography of Red*

How to Trespass
Ralph Waldo Emerson, "Nature"

Raised by Ferns
Margaret Wise Brown, *Fur Family;* Virginia Woolf, "A Room of One's Own"; Immanuel Kant, *Critique of Pure Reason*; W.C. Williams, "Paterson"; Gerard Manley Hopkins, "Pied Beauty" ("plotted and pieced"/ "fickle, freckled"); P. Syme in *Werner's Nomenclature of Colors*; Walt Whitman, *Blades of Grass*; Connie Voisine, "Cameo," "Rosary," and "What Was So Beautiful About the Father," from *Cathedral of the North* (used with permission of the author); Coraline Bickford-Smith's *Fox and Star*; Melissa Kwasny, "Fern"; Inger Christensen, *alphabet* (translated by Susanna Nied); Margery Williams, *The Velveteen Rabbit*; Steven Millhauser, "In the Reign of Harad IV"; Annie Dillard, *The Writing Life*

MAYA JEWELL ZELLER's work has appeared in *The Rumpus, Brevity,* and the *New York Times*-lauded anthology *This is the Place: Women Writing About Home.* Her recent books include *out takes/glove box,* which Eduardo Corral selected as winner of the New American Poetry Prize; and the nonfiction title, *The Wonder of Mushrooms.* Maya teaches poetry and nature writing for Western Colorado University's low-residency MFA program, and writing across genres for Central Washington University's Professional and Creative Writing Program. She lives with her two teens, two tuxedo cats, and ever-expanding library of books in Spokane and Ellensburg.

www.ingramcontent.com/pod-product-compliance
Lightning Source LLC
LaVergne TN
LVHW041625060526
838200LV00040B/1438